2009

2009

Christmas in Spain
and Its Capital, Madrid

The lighting of the municipal Christmas tree heralds the beginning of the Christmas season in Barakaldo, in the Basque region of northern Spain.

Christmas in Spain
and Its Capital, Madrid

Christmas Around the World
From World Book

World Book, Inc.
a Scott Fetzer company
Chicago

Staff

Executive Committee

President
Paul A. Gazzolo

Vice President and Chief Marketing Officer
Patricia Ginnis

Vice President and Chief Financial Officer
Donald D. Keller

Vice President and Editor in Chief
Paul A. Kobasa

Vice President, Licensing & Business Development
Richard Flower

Managing Director, International
Benjamin Hinton

Director, Human Resources
Bev Ecker

Chief Technology Officer
Tim Hardy

Marketing

Director, Direct Marketing
Mark R. Willy

Marketing Analyst
Zofia Kulik

Marketing and Print Promotions Manager
Marco Morales

Editorial

Associate Director, Supplementary Publications
Scott Thomas

Managing Editor, Supplementary Publications
Barbara A. Mayes

Manager, Research, Supplementary Publications
Cheryl Graham

Senior Editor
Kristina Vaicikonis

*Manager, Contracts & Compliance
(Rights & Permissions)*
Loranne K. Shields

Administrative Assistant
Ethel Matthews

*Editorial Administration Director,
Systems and Projects*
Tony Tills

Senor Manager, Publishing Operations
Timothy Falk

Associate Manager, Publishing Operations
Audrey Casey

Graphics and Design

Manager
Tom Evans

Coordinator, Design Development and Production
Brenda B. Tropinski

Associate Designer
Matt Carrington

Photographs Editor
Kathryn Creech

Manager, Cartographic Services
Wayne K. Pichler

Production

Director, Manufacturing and Pre-Press
Carma Fazio

Manufacturing Manager
Steven K. Hueppchen

Production/Technology Manager
Anne Fritzinger

Production Specialist
Curley Hunter

Proofreader
Emilie Schrage

The editors wish to thank the many associations and private individuals in Spain and the United States who took part in developing this book. Special recognition goes to the staff of the Spanish National Tourist Office in Chicago—in particular to Cheryl Kiick and Luis González—for their enthusiasm and invaluable assistance in all phases of the project.

Special appreciation also goes to Julio Albi, Counselor of Cultural Affairs of the Spanish Embassy in Washington, D.C. For their generous advice and assistance, thanks go to Marina A. Seme and Bertha de la Mata.

Carols from THE INTERNATIONAL BOOK OF CHRISTMAS CAROLS by Walter Ehret and translated from the Spanish by George K. Evans. Copyright © 1963, 1970 by Walter Ehret and George K. Evans. Reproduced by permission of Waltr Ehret.

World Book, Inc.
233 N. Michigan Ave.
Chicago, IL 60601
U.S.A.

Library of Congress Cataloging-in-Publication Data
Christmas in Spain and its capital, Madrid.
   p. cm. -- (Christmas around the world)
   Summary: "Customs and traditions of the Christmas holidays as celebrated in Spain and its capital, Madrid. Includes crafts, recipes, and carols"--Provided by publisher.
   ISBN: 978-0-7166-0814-1
   1. Christmas--Spain--Madrid. 2. Madrid (Spain)--Social life and customs. I. World Book, Inc.
   GT4987.61.C482 2009
   394.26630946'41--dc22
                    2009020320

Printed in the United States of America by RR Donnelley, Willard, Ohio
1st printing November 2009

Contents

Spain Prepares for Christmas

*T*hroughout Spain—from the snowy Pyrenees Mountains in the north to sunny Andalusia in the south and from the nation's capital, Madrid, to the smallest town—a sense of excitement builds as the Christmas season approaches. In Spain, the Christmas holidays include not one but three celebrations—Christmas Eve, Christmas Day, and the Day of the Three Kings (January 6)—each with its own special customs and activities.

Spain is a country of great regional differences. On the northeastern border, the mountains called the Pyrenees separate the Iberian Peninsula (which includes Spain and Portugal) from France. The southernmost tip of Spain lies only about 8 miles (13 kilometers) from the northern coast of Africa, across the Strait of Gibraltar.

The official language of Spain is Castilian Spanish, taught in the schools and spoken by most of the people. But in certain northern provinces, a second language is used in addition to Castilian Spanish. In Catalonia, the northeasternmost province, which includes the city of Barcelona, many people speak Catalan, a language similar to the Provençal of southern France, just over the Pyrenees. The Basque people in north-central Spain have their own tongue, a language with no known relations: Basque, also known as Euskera. In northwestern Galicia, a province just north of Portugal, most people speak a Portuguese dialect known as Galician.

Because climate and even language may differ markedly from one region of the country to another, it is not surprising that Christmas observances also vary considerably from region to region. Even within a particular province, Christmas customs and traditions in small towns and villages often have a different character and tone from activities in the larger cities.

Spaniards from the northern regions are likely to decorate their homes with mistletoe and holly as the Nativity approaches, while southerners celebrate with geraniums and heliotrope. The plant life of the two regions reflects the striking climatic difference between them. A white Christmas is not unusual in the Pyrenees or the mountains of Galicia in the northwest. But a Christmas snowfall in Málaga or Cádiz on the southern coast would cause quite a sensation.

The cultures of the north and south are as different as their climates. Spain under Muslim rule for some 700 years before Ferdinand and Isabella drove the last of the Muslim kings from Granada in 1492. For centuries, the north—a center of Visigothic resistance to Muslim rule—evolved primarily under the influence of Roman/European civilizations. Although the Muslim rulers were tolerant of Christianity, the celebration of Christmas tended to be downplayed in southern Spain.

Roman Catholicism has exerted a unifying influence over the various regions of Spain since the Muslim King Muhammad XII went into exile in what is now Morocco

Regions of Spain

◀ *A scene from the Nativity is recreated in the jewel-toned panes of a stained-glass window at the church of Santa Eulalia in Barcelona.*

A colorful outdoor market in Barcelona draws crowds of eager Christmas shoppers.

in 1492. But even the strong hold of Spanish Catholicism has not obliterated regional differences in Spain. For most people, the celebration of Christmas reflects historical and cultural traditions.

Religious observance of the feast of the Nativity is more pronounced in the rural areas than in the cities of Spain. Similarly, one is more likely to come across traditional and distinctly Spanish Christmas customs and practices in small towns and villages than in Madrid, the capital and other bustling metropolitan centers.

Spain has gradually adopted many American and northern European Christmas customs, especially in the large cities. This development probably reflects the rapid economic expansion that transformed Spain after the death of Fascist dictator Francisco Franco in 1975.

Occasionally, one may see a *Papa Noel* (Santa Claus) roaming the streets of Madrid, Barcelona, or one of the other major cities. Although the idea of Santa as a Christmas gift bringer is now fairly widespread in urban Spain, his presence in the pre-Christmas season is not nearly as universal as it is in the United States.

Traditionally, *los Reyes Magos* (the Three Kings) delight Spanish children with holiday presents. And in many families, gifts are still exchanged exclusively on Three Kings' Day (January 6) and are intended primarily for the children. However, the exchange of gifts on Christmas Eve or Christmas Day is becoming increasingly common among some urban Spaniards.

Many city families have adopted the custom of putting up a Christmas tree—a practice that originated in northern Europe. People who live in apartments place the family tree outdoors on the apartment balcony rather than inside. Large condominium complexes will often erect a huge community tree, decorated with electric lights, in the common outdoor courtyard area. Traditional Christmas wreaths decorate the doors of many Spanish homes. Candles and Christmas greenery are also typical decorations.

The Christmas markets

*A*round mid-December, outdoor Christmas markets begin to fill the streets of the old quarters in most Spanish towns, with vendors selling decorations, ornaments, Nativity-scene figures, candy, toys, and gifts. In Madrid, stalls are set up in the vast and beautiful Plaza Mayor. Completed in 1620 during the reign of Philip III (1578-1621), this historic square

Cibeles fountain, a symbol of Madrid, reflects the sparkle of holiday lights in the Plaza de Cibeles as the city prepares for Christmas.

has served as the site of bullfights, masked balls, fireworks displays, the burning of heretics, and the canonization of several saints. In the summer, the Plaza Mayor hosts occasional theatrical performances. But in December, the cobblestones ring with the sounds of merchants setting up their stalls for the holiday season. And in Barcelona, throughout December, the Santa Llúcia fair surrounds the cathedral, filling the narrow streets of the oldest part of the city, known as the Gothic Quarter.

The typical Spanish Christmas market is a riot of color. Christmas ornaments of every size, shape, and hue compete for the shoppers' attention, as well as for their *euros* (the European common currency used in Spain). Some of the stalls feature row upon row of colored plastic balls—the most prevalent decoration by far, and certainly among the cheapest. Stars for the treetop twinkle and glitter next to colorful garlands of tinsel. One vendor might specialize in shiny ribbons for decorating trees and tying up holiday packages. Another might offer handmade ornaments of wood or straw.

The American influence is easy to spot on shelf after shelf of Santa Claus figures and strings of electric lights. Inexpensive toys of almost every description are imported from many other countries as well.

The markets also sell supplies for making *Nacimientos* or *Belenes* (Bethlehems), the crèches, or Nativity scenes, that are found in almost every Spanish home at Christmastime. There are sheets of cork for constructing a stable or cave and moss on which tiny sheep or camels can graze. Miniature figures of the Holy Family, the Three Kings, and animals of every description abound.

Families carefully consider their purchase of a tree in markets that spring up in cities and towns throughout Spain during the month before Christmas.

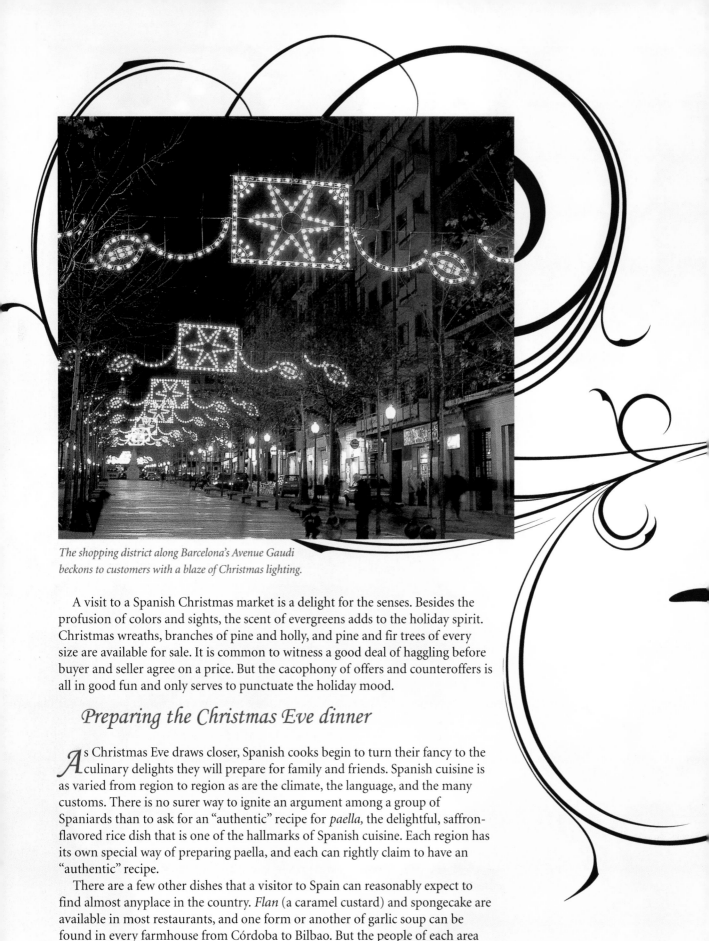

The shopping district along Barcelona's Avenue Gaudi beckons to customers with a blaze of Christmas lighting.

A visit to a Spanish Christmas market is a delight for the senses. Besides the profusion of colors and sights, the scent of evergreens adds to the holiday spirit. Christmas wreaths, branches of pine and holly, and pine and fir trees of every size are available for sale. It is common to witness a good deal of haggling before buyer and seller agree on a price. But the cacophony of offers and counteroffers is all in good fun and only serves to punctuate the holiday mood.

Preparing the Christmas Eve dinner

As Christmas Eve draws closer, Spanish cooks begin to turn their fancy to the culinary delights they will prepare for family and friends. Spanish cuisine is as varied from region to region as are the climate, the language, and the many customs. There is no surer way to ignite an argument among a group of Spaniards than to ask for an "authentic" recipe for *paella*, the delightful, saffron-flavored rice dish that is one of the hallmarks of Spanish cuisine. Each region has its own special way of preparing paella, and each can rightly claim to have an "authentic" recipe.

There are a few other dishes that a visitor to Spain can reasonably expect to find almost anyplace in the country. *Flan* (a caramel custard) and spongecake are available in most restaurants, and one form or another of garlic soup can be found in every farmhouse from Córdoba to Bilbao. But the people of each area

In rural areas, the smell of roasting chestnuts tempts homeward-bound villagers during the pre-Christmas season.

have their own way of preparing these foods and often wrinkle their noses at the way certain dishes are cooked in neighboring provinces. The Andalusians dislike the Catalan taste for sweets with meats, and, in turn, the Catalans find the peppery food of the Estremadurans thoroughly disagreeable. One food writer summed up the argument by dubbing Spanish cooking a "regional cuisine with national characteristics."

Despite regional differences, there are certain foods that are customarily served at Christmastime in almost every part of Spain. The traditional Christmas Eve dinner table is filled with such dishes as seafood from Galicia, almond or garlic soup, roasted lamb or capon or turkey stuffed with truffles, broiled sea bream with potatoes, green beans, dried fruit and nuts, a wide assortment of traditional Christmas sweets, as well as wine and liqueurs.

In a number of convents in the city of Seville, cloistered nuns have prepared Christmas pastries and sweets for centuries. This tradition dates back to the 1200's at the time of the Reconquest of Muslim kingdoms—with the exception of Granada—by Christian King Fernando III (1217-1252) and the founding of convents and monasteries. The nuns made the holiday sweets for their benefactors, mostly noble families and feudal lords. The Monastery of Santa Clara, established in 1295, produces *yemas,* confections made of egg yolks, sugar, and lemon. The legacy of this culinary art, however, dates back much further. The Moors introduced the elaborate sweet doughs made of almonds, eggs, and honey. Many of these pastries are made with olive oil instead of *lard* (pork fat), because Arabs did not eat pork.

In Estepa, 68 miles (109 kilometers) west of Seville, from September to January, the entire village is filled with the aroma of the sweet almond dough used to make *mantecados.* For it is here that 2,000 people— about one-sixth of the population—work in the 30 mantecado factories, which produce 44 million pounds (19.9 million kilograms) of the pastries every year.

Shared traditions, with a regional touch

*F*eliz Navidad (literally, "Happy Christmas") is the standard greeting of one Spaniard to another as Christmas Eve approaches. In the larger cities, streets and major squares are gaily decorated with electric lights and other ornaments. Department stores display their wares beneath banners expressing that most universal of Christmas sentiments: *Paz en la Tierra a los Hombres de Buena Voluntad*—"Peace on Earth to People of Good Will."

El Cant dels Ocells
(Carol of the Birds)

A 19th century card provides Christmas greetings from the distributor of Barcelona's daily La Vanguardia. *The sending of Christmas cards was particularly popular among tradespeople, who sent cards to valued clients.*

Upon this holy night,
When God's great star appears,
And floods the earth with brightness,
Birds' voices rise in song,
And, warbling all night long,
Express their glad hearts' lightness.

The Nightingale is first
To bring his song of cheer,
And tell us of his gladness:
"Jesus, our Lord, is born
To free us from all sin,
And banish ev'ry sadness."

The answ'ring Sparrow cries:
"God comes to earth this day
Amid the angels flying."
Trilling in sweetest tones,
The Finch his Lord now owns:
"To Him be all thanksgiving."

The Partridge adds his note:
"To Bethlehem I'll fly,
Where in the stall He's lying.
There, near the manger blest,
I'll build myself a nest,
And sing my love undying."

The excitement of the approaching festivities is just as great in rural areas. Here, electric Christmas lights illuminate village footpaths as chestnut vendors roast their wares for homebound shepherds, farmers, and shopkeepers.

No significant event takes place in Spain without being celebrated in song and dance—least of all *la Navidad,* or Christmas. As one might expect, there is as much variety in costume, music, and styles of dancing from region to region as there is in climate and cuisine. One generalization that can be made, however, is that the music represents Spain's Roman Catholic majority. For example, "El Cant dels Ocells"(the "Carol of the Birds"), which originated in Catalonia, tells the story of the Nativity from the point of view of the birds that witnessed the event. Like the shepherd from whose imagination they sprang, the birds in the carol are clearly well versed in the Roman Catholic faith.

The custom of exchanging Christmas cards is common in both rural and urban areas. The cards typically feature reproductions of paintings of the Nativity or the Three Kings, though cards with more secular holiday graphics and greetings are also available.

In certain areas, various service and tradespeople will present cards—similar to calling cards—to their customers with such greetings as, "Your postal worker wishes you a Happy Holiday Season." In return, the customer presents a cash gift. One travel writer describes a police officer directing traffic in Ávila on the day before Christmas enclosed in a waist-high wall of hams, cheeses, fruits, and wineskins—all presents from the good citizens of his district.

Large commercial organizations—banks, corporations, and the like—often send huge, elaborate baskets of liquor, fruit, and sweets to important clients. Shops and delis in the larger cities sometimes feature these baskets in display windows. Curious shoppers enjoy looking the baskets over, but they are not the sort of present most Spaniards would give to a friend or relative.

Mazapán

Among the many sweets available in Spain at Christmastime, none is molded into more fantastic guises than marzipan, an Arabic delicacy that the Spanish know as *mazapán*. Made of crushed almonds (another introduction from Muslims), plus sugar and eggs, Spanish marzipan has such distinctive qualities that many say it is the best in the world.

Toledo is the mazapán capital of Spain. The city is as well known for its sweets as it is for the keen blades it produces for bullfighting. The nuns of the convents of Jesús y María of San Clemente and of Santo Domingo el Antiguo have been making mazapán for centuries, as numerous family-owned businesses have for generations.

Connoisseurs of Spanish mazapán can discuss its fine points for hours on end. Do the best almonds come from Andalusia in the south? Yes, say some. Others, however, insist that the finest almonds in the world come from south of Valencia, along the Mediterranean coast.

Spanish mazapán can be shaped into balls, or ovals, or sometimes into little cups and filled with apricot jam. But at Christmastime, Toledo's masters and mistresses of mazapán let their imaginations run wild. The candy is formed into utterly fantastic shapes. Long lengths of mazapán are coiled into round boxes and decorated to look like eels or dragons. With sugar scales, candy eyes, and almond-studded jaws, these toothsome monsters are shipped all over Spain, and as far as the United States, to delight and amaze children of all ages.

A shop window in Toledo, the mazapán capital of Spain, displays the crushed-almond delicacy in every imaginable form.

A Nacimiento artisan proudly displays wares at an open-air Christmas market. Nacimiento figures have a place of honor in Spanish homes during the Christmas season.

Setting up the Nacimiento

*I*n every house in Spain—especially those with children—the universal pre-Christmas activity is the construction of the family *Nacimiento,* the Nativity scene. Many families buy the necessary figures, but most make their own setting—a cave or stable, and a background that may be as simple as shepherds on a hillside or as elaborate as a re-creation of the entire town of Bethlehem. Children and adults alike spend much time on this family project.

A typical family Nacimiento will include the figures of Mary, Joseph, and the infant Jesus, plus the Three Kings, some shepherds, and an angel announcing the birth of Christ. These are the basics. Many Nacimientos, however, are much more elaborate. The Kings' entourage may feature a number of servants, plus camels, donkeys, or whatever transportation the family decides befits such a royal party. A river of aluminum foil is a common background feature, with one or more women doing laundry and perhaps a couple of people fishing. Some Nacimientos even include the castle of King Herod and the figures of Roman soldiers.

At urban Christmas markets, one can purchase entire families of miniature animals to place in the Nacimiento—sow and piglets, cow and calf, hen and chicks, and more. With so many city families living in small apartments, most urban Nacimientos are scaled to fit a compact space. But in larger homes or public places, Nacimientos may be much larger, even life-sized.

Some schools and churches have living Nacimientos. Students or parishioners assume the various roles in the Nativity scene. Some groups use Nacimientos as fundraising vehicles.

Belenistas are individuals who make Nacimientos. They and anyone who wants to promote Nacimientos often form organizations that display them. The groups may also sponsor competitions in which awards are given to the best Nacimiento in a particular year.

As the Advent season draws to a close, Spaniards exchange holiday greetings, busy themselves with the family Nacimiento, and otherwise prepare for Christmas Eve, fully savoring the pleasure of anticipation. Along city streets and village lanes, spirits rise as steadily as the Christmas star.

El Gordo

Throughout Spain, in the final days before Christmas, young and old eagerly look forward to a tradition that began in 1763—the national lottery, or Loteria Nacional. King Charles III (1716-1788) began the national lottery system to fund charity; however, over the years, it became a way to raise money for the government. Now, about 70 percent of lottery sales are paid out in winnings, and 30 percent are kept by the government.

The lottery held on December 22 is called *El Gordo,* literally, "the Fat One." It is billed as one of the largest lotteries in Europe. (A smaller lottery that takes place on January 6, the feast of the Epiphany, is known as El Niño.) El Gordo has taken place every year since 1812. The drawing is unusual in that its aim is not to have a single winner, but rather to allow millions of people to share the wealth.

Most people cannot afford to buy a single ticket by themselves. In 2008, for example, a ticket cost $263. Rather, individuals buy tenths of a ticket, sharing tickets with co-workers, family members, and friends. So each ticket, which has one preprinted, five-digit number and is decorated with a Nativity scene, is sold in tenths. In addition, each ticket number is sold in a series or set, so that a single number may be repeated in more than 100 sets. If that number is chosen, all of the hundreds or thousands of people who bought parts of that ticket series win a share of the money. One year, all 350 inhabitants of a small village shared in a $6-million prize.

The drawing for the winning El Gordo numbers begins at 9 a.m. and is broadcast live nationwide over radio, television, and Internet. By tradition, children chosen for their singing ability from the Saint Ildefonso School in Madrid (which was once an orphanage) draw numbers and prizes from two giant gold drums. One child draws and then sings out a number, while the other draws and sings out the prize that holders of that ticket will share. And then the winners spill out into the streets throughout Spain, celebrating their good fortune!

An official releases the balls in preparation for drawing the winning numbers of El Gordo, the Spanish Christmas lottery. El Gordo—literally, the Fat One—takes place on December 22 each year, in a tradition that dates back to 1812. The televised drawing brings the nation to a standstill as Spaniards young and old eagerly check their tickets.

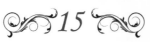

A Spanish Christmas: Revelry and Reverence

*C*hristmas in Spain is a festival that blends the religious spirit of the Nativity with the delights of the table, and the Spanish passion for song and dance with the universal pleasure of renewing family ties. The Spanish Christmas Eve is known as *Nochebuena,* the "good night." It is a time of gaiety and merrymaking. Early in the day, everyone who can do so hurries forth into the streets. In cities and villages, people browse through the markets for last-minute purchases of food, decorations, and increasingly, presents.

In village markets, turkeys that escaped Advent grocery shopping gobble forlornly from stacked cages. Quacking ducks and cooing pigeons help to swell the sounds of Christmas. Towering piles of golden Valencia oranges, luscious dates, and olives, which are indispensable to any Spanish feast, overwhelm display shelves. Scattered among them are cheeses of every conceivable variety, quaint pigskins of wine, and choice candies from many parts of Spain.

Every region seems to have its own sweetmeat or pastry specialty. In all but the smallest towns and villages, however, *pastelerías* (pastry shops) and tearooms offer an extraordinary variety of *dulces* (sweets): plump, sugar-coated fruits; cream- or custard-filled cakes; and pastries oozing with jam.

Pineapples from the Azores, bananas from the Canary Islands, melons, oranges, pears, plums, and other fresh fruits are the usual mealtime desserts in Spain. Still, there seems to be a constant demand for dulces, and never more so than at Christmastime. (The Azores are a group of mid-Atlantic islands that belong to Portugal; the Canary Islands, off the west coast of Morocco, belong to Spain.)

Over a cup of tea, coffee, or the thick, rich chocolate that is so popular in Spain, Iberians take time out from preparing for the onslaught of distant relatives to relish a cake or pastry and wish friends and neighbors the joys of the season. The tearooms and cafes of Spain are places to congregate between lunch and dinner and share the events of the day with friends.

The universal Christmas treat in Spain is *turrón,* a kind of nougat made with toasted almonds, sugar, honey, and eggs. Like many traditional Spanish foods, turrón comes in several varieties, qualities, and prices. Some forms melt in one's mouth; others have the consistency of peanut brittle, hard and almost rocklike.

Historians differ in their accounts of the origin of turrón. Some trace the tradition back a thousand years before the time of Christ, when Carthaginians came to the Iberian Peninsula from Asia Minor. They offered gifts in the form of cakes to one of their goddesses, the Lady Baalat.

Other historians suggest that the giving of turrón may date back to the Roman custom of exchanging sweetmeats at the January *calends* (first day of the month), to ensure that the coming year might be full of sweetness. But no matter how the custom began, people in Spain look forward to eating turrón at Christmastime.

◄ *Reverent shepherds grace the façade of Barcelona's La Sagrada Familia (church of the Holy Family), designed by famed Barcelona architect Antonio Gaudí (1852-1926).*

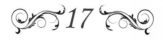

Colorful zambombas, which come in all sizes, are traditional Spanish folk instruments that are widely used to accompany the singing of Christmas carols.

Regional favorites also play an important role in satisfying the Spanish sweet tooth during the Christmas holidays. In rural Aragon, an almond caramel called *guirlache* is a popular way to top off the Nochebuena meal. Various sections of the Asturias are famous for their tarts. *Escaldau,* made from corn, rye flour, honey, and butter, is served steaming hot, fresh from the oven. *Quesadillas,* folded pastry stuffed with cheese, fruit, or sometimes nuts, are another Asturian favorite.

The Nochebuena meal

Although the Iberians are justly famous for their hospitality, the Nochebuena meal and the Christmas day meal are generally reserved for the immediate and extended family. There are other occasions during the holidays that Spaniards share with friends—notably New Year's Eve. But Christmas is almost exclusively a family affair.

The traditional Nochebuena dinner is an elaborate meal consisting of several courses. Menus vary from province to province, of course, but there are certain recurring themes.

Among some families, visiting relatives will be welcomed by the scent of freshly roasted chestnuts, a fragrance that punctuates the Spanish holidays from Nochebuena all the way through Three Kings' Day. The chestnut grows well in Spain and is a favorite of Spanish palates. Toasted almonds are another popular appetizer, as are olives that have been marinated for several days in olive oil and garlic. The first, or appetizer, course is often rounded out by a selection of fine cheeses, perhaps accompanied by anchovies. All of these "finger foods"—as well as slices of sausage and other meats on bits of bread—are collectively known as *tapas.* In many homes, tapas are accompanied by muscatel, a rich sweet wine, or by a Spanish sherry.

Soup—either chestnut, creamy garlic, or almond—is an optional second course. Whether or not a soup is prepared, most hosts offer a fish course before presenting the main dish of turkey, lamb, or pork.

One traditional Christmas dish, *besugo,* is a Mediterranean sea bream very similar to red snapper. In places where bream is not available, Spanish cooks often substitute flounder. The fish is topped with seasoned breadcrumbs, lightly sprinkled with olive oil, and baked whole, often surrounded by sliced potatoes and onions. Garnished with lemon

Tempting dishes are laid out in preparation for a family's Nochebuena meal. Families usually begin to gather for the Christmas Eve dinner just after nightfall and feast until it is time to leave for midnight Mass.

slices, besugo makes an attractive addition to the holiday table. In Galicia, the fish course is *bacalao,* the dried salt codfish plentiful in that region. First, the fish is tenderized by beating it against a tabletop. Then it is soaked in water at least overnight. The prepared fish is dusted with flour and fried in olive oil with potatoes and onions. The finished creation is brought to the table crowned with parsley and olives and garnished with slices of hard-cooked egg.

Substitutions for the traditional Christmas turkey abound. In Galicia, a suckling pig or meat pie might be served. In rural Aragon, the Christmas Eve meal might include a main course of lamb and chicken. There are also regional variations on turkey. *Madrileños,* that is, the citizens of Madrid, frequently accompany their Christmas turkey with a side dish of red cabbage—*Lombarda de San Isidro.* (The dish is named for San Isidro, the city's patron saint.) Green beans in tomato sauce is another popular favorite. Fresh green beans are lightly sautéed in olive oil and garlic, combined with chopped tomatoes and pine nuts, and seasoned with lemon juice and bay leaf.

The standard way to top off a Nochebuena meal is with a big, rectangular block of turrón (nougat). The block is cut into individual slices for serving. Candy-coated almonds may also be offered, as well as a compote of apples, pears, or mixed fruits.

The dessert is often accompanied by *cava* (KAH vuh) a sparkling wine similar to champagne. Catalonia produces cava, so this beverage is within the means of most Spanish families. In some homes, the hosts may substitute a sparkling cider.

A street performer and puppet vendor entertains holiday crowds in Barcelona.

The family gathers

The Nochebuena meal is, obviously, quite a production, and there always seems to be some forgotten ingredient that has to be purchased at the last minute. As Christmas Eve shoppers hurry through the afternoon sun, they are sped on their way by the sound of guitars, castanets, and other traditional folk instruments. On every other corner, it seems, groups of musicians gather to perform the traditional Spanish carols known as *villancicos*. As often as not, people who pause to listen for a moment or two will join in the refrain.

For centuries it was the custom in Spain to place a lighted oil lamp in a window as soon as dusk fell on Christmas Eve. Many families, especially those living in the countryside, still follow this practice. Religious families may also light candles before the home shrine to the Virgin Mary or place candles around the family Nacimiento.

The influence of the original Spanish settlers is still apparent in certain parts of the southwestern United States, where the practice of setting out *luminarios* (festive lights) on Christmas Eve persists. Luminarios are made by partly filling paper bags with sand and inserting a candle in each bag. The luminarios are placed on rooftops, garden walls, and walkways. They are lighted at dusk on Christmas Eve, and the soft, radiant light is said to guide the Christ child to each home.

After nightfall in Spanish households, aunts, uncles, brothers, sisters, grandparents, and cousins galore begin to arrive. The walls reverberate with the noisy chatter that is typical of most family reunions. The children grow more and more impatient as the house fills with the tempting smells of the Nochebuena dinner. Around 9:00 or 10:00—not an unusual dinner hour in Spain—the family sits down to eat, and the meal continues until it is time for midnight Mass.

At midnight on Christmas Eve, Spaniards flock to Mass to join the priest and choir in welcoming the newborn Christ child.

Midnight Mass

The *Misa del Gallo,* or Mass of the cock's crow, is the only Mass said at midnight the whole year-around. And for the little ones especially, it has an air of great excitement and adventure. Many of them have never before been out so late.

In small towns, everyone will turn out for the midnight Mass, which is a social, as well as a religious, event. People who have moved away frequently travel many miles from their homes in the larger cities to attend Christmas Eve Mass at their native village churches. Everyone in town is curious to see who will show up—and with whom—what new babies have been born, and so on.

Although in big cities social pressure to attend Mass is much less intense, midnight Mass on Christmas Eve is still a widespread custom. For this special occasion, priests put on their most gorgeous robes, some of them worn only on Christmas Eve. The vestments are adorned with rare embroidery, and they sparkle with precious jewels. In the great cathedrals, the rich tones of the organ swell along with the music from guitars, tambourines, and castanets. Priests, choir, and congregation join to sing traditional carols.

The celebration of the midnight Mass in Labastida, in the Basque province of Álava, dates from the Middle Ages. Just before midnight, in

Dolls and stuffed animals in all shapes and sizes attract shoppers to a window display in central Madrid.

front of the Consistorial House (town hall), a dozen shepherds gather to sing for the mayor and town council. Led by an old man carrying a lamb and a shepherdess bearing an image of the infant Jesus, the group sings all the way to church. There they greet the priest and perform a ritual dance that involves beating the floor with sticks. There is singing and dancing all through the Mass.

Afterward, the shepherds build a bonfire near the church and pretend to make some soup, which is offered to the image of the Christ child, still safe in the arms of the shepherdess.

In the Pyrenees, people remember the dead on Christmas Eve. There, it is the custom to leave out a loaf of bread with a knife stuck in it before going to midnight Mass. The loaf has been left as food for loved ones who have died.

After church on Christmas Eve, most Spaniards return home and go to bed. Some, however, continue their Christmas Eve merrymaking until the wee hours of the morning. One traditional lyric sums up the spirit of the occasion: "Long live merrymaking, for this is a day of rejoicing. And may the perfume of pleasure sweeten our existence."

Gift giving on either Christmas Eve or the morning of Christmas Day has become increasingly customary for some families in Spain. These are generally the only times adults exchange gifts. But children may get gifts twice during the season—a small gift from Papa Noel on Christmas and most of their gifts on Three Kings' Day, the traditional and still universal Spanish holiday for the exchange of presents.

Throngs of shoppers enjoy the holiday lights on a busy street in Madrid in the weeks before Christmas.

Such Christmas traditions as stuffing the holiday turkey and grinding almonds for sopa de almendra have not changed much since the 1800's, preserved in a period engraving.

Villagers portray the Holy Family in a living Nativity scene in Ojen, near Málaga, in the province of Andalusia.

The legacy of St. Francis

On Christmas morning, the family Nacimiento becomes the center of attention. The figure of the Christ child is lovingly placed in the manger, and the scene is illuminated by candlelight. The children, often dressed in peasant costumes and playing tambourines, castanets, and other traditional folk instruments, sing and dance to the lilting strains of Spanish villancicos. Once the children have had their chance to perform, everyone joins in singing the beloved carols.

What the Christmas tree is to northern Europe, the Nativity scene is to the south. This Christmas custom is said to have originated in the Middle Ages, and its popularization is most often ascribed to Saint Francis of Assisi, the "Little Brother of Mankind."

During the Middle Ages, there were few books and few people able to read. Masses and church ceremonies were conducted in Latin, and Saint Francis worried, with good reason, that such important holidays as Christmas and Easter held little real meaning for common people. His earnest desire was to humanize the teachings of the Scriptures, to help ordinary people feel the religious experience more deeply by making the story of Christ's birth more accessible.

Legend has it that Saint Francis was inspired to set up a Nativity scene when he saw some shepherds asleep in the fields near Greccio, Italy. It occurred to him that a live reenactment of the arrival of the Savior would help

to make the true significance of the Nativity apparent to all. Saint Francis turned to his close friend, Greccio's wealthy nobleman Giovanni Velita, for assistance.

The event took place in a cave on a hill above Greccio. For weeks, Giovanni's preparations created quite a stir in the town and countryside. The nobleman hired real people to take the parts of Mary, Joseph, and the shepherds, and he commissioned a life-sized wax figure to represent the Christ child. When all the props had been assembled, including a manger, straw, a live ox, and a donkey, Saint Francis himself arranged and directed the scene.

On Christmas Eve in 1223, throngs of worshipers crowded the hillside, many carrying torches and presents for the Holy Infant. Saint Bonaventure described the scene in his biography of Saint Francis, published in 1260. Many witnesses, Bonaventure said, came to understand the meaning of the birth in Bethlehem for the first time. Saint Francis was so delighted that he stood before the manger "bathed in tears and overflowing with joy."

Saint Francis celebrated a solemn Mass and preached a sermon. He begged the people to cleanse their hearts of hatred and to entertain only thoughts of peace during the Christmas season. He also sought to underscore the meaning of the Nativity by pointing out that the Christ child, Savior of the world, was born to parents just as poor as—if not poorer than—the assembled worshipers.

Francis's dramatization made such an impression on the people of Greccio that the practice was repeated Christmas after Christmas. Soon it spread throughout Italy, and from there to Spain, Portugal, France, and the rest of Europe.

Bakers add a final layer of toasted nuts to a batch of turrón. Work begins well in advance to supply enough of the almond and honey nougat, a favorite holiday treat.

The saint led his people in songs of joy. No doubt some of these songs were among the earliest Christmas carols. He encouraged the children who were present to sing around the manger to the baby Jesus. From this custom have come several beautiful lullabies to the Christ child, including a few of the oldest villancicos.

Of course, the modern practice of singing and dancing around the Nacimiento can be traced directly to the event at Greccio. Having concluded their devotions at home, many devout Spanish Catholic families attend one or more of the three Masses that are celebrated on Christmas Day.

Enjoying Christmas Day

The main meal of the day is taken around the middle of the afternoon and, like the Nochebuena dinner, is shared with members of the extended family. The Christmas dinner is generally as elaborate as the previous day's, with a main course of roast turkey, goose, or capon. *Puchero olla*—a special dish made of chicken, beef, mutton, bacon, pigs' feet, and garlic—may also be featured. The meal is accompanied by plenty of wine —Spanish families reserve their best vintages for the holiday season—and topped off with the ever-present turrón.

The traditional rite of the Urn of Fate is a practice that has survived since the days when Roman troops occupied the Iberian Peninsula. In

Naughty tiós de Nadal (Yule logs) are part of a popular Christmas tradition for children in the province of Catalan. Throughout December, the children "feed" the tiós candies, nuts, dried fruit, and trinkets. On Christmas Day, they beat the tió with sticks until the log releases its treasures, to be shared by all.

many communities, the names of friends and neighbors are written on cards and placed in a giant bowl. With much laughter and merriment, the cards are drawn two at a time, to see who fate has determined must become special friends during the following year.

In some communities, this old folkway is a kind of matchmaking ceremony, and names in the bowl may be shamelessly maneuvered by interested parties to achieve the desired results. The outcome is sometimes disappointing, but everyone grins and bears it.

Youngsters in Cádiz perform another rite that dates from pagan times, "swing in the sun." Swings are set up in the public squares, and the children compete to see who can go highest in the air, thus helping the sun on its return journey northward. The custom is a modern-day reminder that the feast of Christmas has its origins in ancient celebrations of the winter solstice.

Catalonian villagers have their own colorful ways of celebrating the Christmas holidays. Families set up a hollowed out Yule log, or *tió de Nadal*, in their home. The log stands on little stick legs, has a friendly face painted on it, and wears a sock hat reminiscent of a traditional Catalan peasant hat called a *barretina*. Each night beginning on December 8, the children feed candy, nuts, dried fruit, and trinkets into a hole in the log and cover the hole with burlap or a rag. By December 25, the log is stuffed. On Christmas Day, the children beat the log with sticks to make it

A larger-than-life Nativity scene is one of many in the squares of towns and villages across Spain in the weeks before Christmas. St. Francis of Assisi is credited with setting up the first Nativity scene, in Greccio, Italy, in 1223.

"poop" its treasures as they sing traditional songs. The gifts are shared by all. According to tradition, the "pooping log" ensures prosperity and luck in the coming year by "fertilizing" the earth, a reference to Spain's agrarian past.

In the Basque region, in the shadow of the Pyrenees, Christmas is traditionally celebrated with song. A few days before Christmas, Basque children dress up as peasants and parade along the streets of their village with Olentzero. Olentzero is a mythical peasant who spends the rest of the year in the mountains making charcoal for the villagers to heat their homes. He is a fat, jolly man who likes to drink wine and smoke a pipe. As the children march down the streets carrying a life-like image of Olentzero, they stop frequently to sing loud, funny songs about their imaginary friend and collect sweets from the villagers. In some villages, a man dresses up like Olentzero and passes out logs to make sure no one is cold at Christmas. On Christmas Eve, and continuing through December 31, Olentzero is said to journey from one Basque village to another, delivering gifts to his young friends.

By the close of Christmas Day, the newborn Christ child has been royally welcomed throughout Spain, according to the custom in each region. Family ties have been renewed, and the joys of the Nativity celebrated by sharing the finest available food and wine.

But the festivities are not yet over. For the children, especially, the best is yet to come as they look forward with mounting impatience to the arrival of the Three Kings.

The Songs and Dances of Spanish Christmas

University students in traditional dress entertain visitors with lively villancicos at the cathedral in Santiago de Compostela in the province of Galicia. Roving groups of Spanish students, called tunas, have performed the carols in the month before Christmas for centuries.

◄ Saint Cecilia, the patron saint of music, plays a clavichord, a predecessor of the piano, in a painting by Flemish artist Michiel van Coxcie (1499-1592) at the Museo del Prado in Madrid.

*R*egional folk songs and dances add a special touch to the Christmas season in Spain. As one might expect, the celebration of the Nativity in song and dance varies as much from province to province as does the Spanish climate and cuisine. Yet the love of pageantry and music is nationwide—with roots that, in many instances, can be traced back to the late Middle Ages.

Christianity was the dominant cultural force throughout Spain and western Europe from about 1100 to 1500. The late Middle Ages saw the spread of a wide variety of Christmas celebrations through all levels of society. Masses were celebrated in the impressive Gothic cathedrals, built as monuments to the religious fervor of kings, monks, and artists. Simpler religious pageants, reflecting the humbler faith of the common people, were also staged.

The celebration of Christmas had its secular side as well—a side that grew in gaiety and abandon as the period progressed. The feast of the Nativity included organized horseplay among ordinary citizens and ritual contests held by plumed and armor-coated knights. Riotous processions and elaborate pantomimes were capped by noisy songfests.

Christmas carols first appeared in western Europe during the late Middle Ages (1300's to 1400's). Stately Christmas hymns, sung in Latin, had graced Nativity Masses for centuries. These solemn verses, however, focused on the theological implications of the Incarnation. The carols, expressing the simple human emotion of joy at the birth of a Savior, were distinctly different.

The first carols were simple, homely verses set to dance tunes, which until the 1300's had been secular in theme, celebrating love, courtship, the joys of spring, or other cheerful subject matter. Beginning around 1400, Spanish and other western European composers began to adapt these secular dancing songs for religious

A Spanish Christmas hymn is preserved in a manuscript dating from before the adoption of the Gregorian calendar (1582) at the Cathedral of León, France.

purposes—specifically, to express the popular belief and joy in humanity's salvation that lie at the heart of Christmas. Many Spanish carols that are still sung today had their origins in this movement and date from the 1400's and 1500's.

Throughout this period, the gaiety and abandon of the Christmas holidays increased. Those who could afford to dressed and dined lavishly. By the mid-1400's, Spaniards were dancing in churches as well as in the streets—a practice that persists to this day.

Songs of the tunas

The *tunas* have inherited this centuries-old tradition. These bands of university students sing and play music for the entertainment and the coins of holiday tourists. Their festive *traje*, or costume, has remained the same for hundreds of years: black velvet doublet, knee breeches, cloak if the weather is chilly, white neck-ruff or collar, and long, brightly colored sashes.

The Spanish word *tuno*, literally translated, means a rogue or wanderer, and today's young musicians do their best to live up to their name. They wander through the streets, restaurants, bars, and hotel lobbies at night, serenading onlookers. They sing traditional songs to the accompaniment of guitars and tambourines, and sometimes even dance—all to coax their admirers into giving them money, wine, and sweets.

In Seville, tunas are the first to usher in the Spanish Christmas holidays. Just before midnight on December 7, all of the tunas in the city—and many from all over Spain—gather at the statue of the Virgin Mary. Their serenade precedes the festivities that will take place on the next day, the Feast of the Immaculate Conception.

Dance of the Sixes

On December 8, a group of youngsters continues yet another centuries-old tradition—the famous *Danza de los Seises* (Dance of the Sixes) at the Seville Cathedral. This impressive ceremony takes place in the morning of the feast day. Flags fly in the streets, flowers bedeck apartment balconies, and candles are lit in windows throughout the city.

As the morning sun washes the streets of Seville with a pinkish-orange glow, people from all over Spain, and from many foreign countries, begin to assemble in the cathedral. The Dance of the Sixes is performed by 10 choirboys before the main altar. (Although the number of participants has been expanded to 10 over the years, the dance is still known by its original name.)

The choirboys are dressed in the fashion of page boys of the 1400's, a costume of pale blue satin trimmed in lace, complete with plumed, wide-brimmed hats. The morning sun illuminates the cathedral's immense rose windows and casts shadows across the ancient stone floor. Banks of candles flicker from the silver high altar, creating a glowing aura. It is a Rembrandt-like setting, rich in light and shadow.

Since dancing in all its forms is so much a part of the life and spirit of the Spanish people, this stunning and reverent ceremony is as natural as it is memorable. The ceremony begins with a simple hymn, sung by the choirboys to the accompaniment of organ and orchestra:

Choirboys perform the spectacular Dance of the Sixes before the Seville cathedral altar, an event that inaugurates the Christmas season in that city.

With the sharp staccato roll of castanets echoing across the cavernous cathedral, the boys sing and whirl through a triumphant conclusion. They kneel and bow to the altar, and the dance is ended.

Spanish folk instruments

The songs and dances of a Spanish Christmas generally are performed to the accompaniment of one or more traditional folk instruments. More elaborate instrumentation may also be employed, as in the Dance of the Sixes or the impressive midnight Masses in the larger cathedrals. But even then, the booming sound of the organ or the woodwinds and brass of a full orchestra will be punctuated with the wooden clack of castanets or the strum of one or more guitars.

Two of the easiest folk instruments to play—and, therefore, the most common—are the tambourine and the *sonaja*. The latter is a round percussion instrument similar to the tambourine and made of rows of wire or thin strips of tin. These are strung with pairs of small tin disks.

The *zambomba* is another instrument that frequently accompanies the songs of carolers. It consists of a cylinder, approximately 10 inches (25 centimeters) high, with a skin stretched taut across the top to form a sort of drum. A lightweight stick is inserted through the bottom of the cylinder and pushed through a hole in the skin. The top of the stick projects upward and is often decorated with ribbons or colored paper flowers.

The zambomba may look like a drum, but it is not played like a drum or any other instrument. Instead of beating on the drumlike head, the player spits on his hand and moves the oiled stick up and down, producing a steady, rhythmic wail.

In northwest Spain, the *gaita* (bagpipe) is as purely Spanish as castanets are in the south. The people of Asturias and Galicia trace their heritage back to the Celts (ancient inhabitants of parts of Europe, including Great Britain and Ireland), a heritage that is apparent in the music, dances, and folklore of the region. Because the mountain ranges and heavy rains in northwestern Spain prevented the Moors from gaining a foothold there, the Galicians and Asturians still think of themselves as "pure" Spaniards. To the rest of the world, however, their Celtic temperament, a kind of lyrical, nostalgic melancholy, makes them as different from their fellow Spaniards as winter is from summer.

Ay, Jesús mío,
tu amor me inflame;
Ay, ay, Jesús mío,
tu amor me inflame;
Pues ha salido para inflamarme!
Ven, amor mío;
ven, y no tardes;
ven como sueles a consolarme!

Oh, my Jesus,
Your love inflames me.
Surely you have come to inspire me.
Come, precious Lord;
Come, don't delay;
Come, be my source
Of consolation.

As the dance begins, the hymn is repeated.

The movements of the Dance of the Sixes have been compared with those of many other dances—ranging from the minuet to the performances of Japanese geishas. But the dance is, in fact, unique. Imbued with the spirit of Roman Catholicism, each figure—the star, the wheel, the double chain—has a religious significance. The "SS" of the double chain, for example, represents the *Santísimo Sacramento,* most holy sacrament.

Hundreds of people gather in front of the cathedral in Barcelona to dance the sardana.

Dances of the regions

*M*any traditional northwestern dances, from the *vaqueira*, a kind of formal herders' dance, to the freewheeling *pericote*, are performed to the drone of the bagpipe. These dances contrast sharply with the more familiar flamenco of Andalusia to the south.

No Andalusian Christmas would be complete without the fierce stamping of feet and rattling of castanets that characterize the flamenco—a fiery, passionate dance, strongly suggestive of Moorish influence. The emotional *cante hondo* often begins with a long, drawn-out, ear-piercing cry, like that of the Muslim *muezzin* calling the faithful to prayer from atop a high minaret. The music is usually performed on a guitar; the underlying beat is emphasized by the rhythmic clapping of hands and snapping of fingers.

The merry, yet understated, Catalan *sardana* could hardly be more different from the sensual flamenco. An ensemble of pipes, flutes, trumpets, and other wind instruments, rather than the guitar, usually accompanies this dance. While the flamenco is danced singly or by couples, the sardana is performed by large groups arranged in circles. Believed to be of Greek origin, the dance looks remarkably like a Greek folk dance—a happy, floating circle of dancers, moving and turning as one. Compared with the fiery flamenco, the sardana seems almost emotionless, yet graceful and effortless.

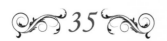

Awaiting the Three Kings

*T*he passing of Christmas ushers in another phase of the holiday season —the long wait for the arrival of the Three Kings. These traditional gift bearers of the Spanish Christmas season do not distribute their presents until January 6, also known as the Feast of the Epiphany. The interval between December 25 and the Feast of the Epiphany constitutes the Twelve Days of Christmas—a period decidedly more secular in tone than the week or two before Christmas. Families spend a good deal of time window-shopping and browsing through stores, so that the children can decide what they would like to ask the Kings to bring.

Dolls, stuffed animals, toy cars and trucks—these perennial favorites retain their appeal. But nowadays, they compete for children's attention with the latest electronic games, toy robots, interactive books, and other modern-day attractions.

There may be a good deal of agonizing over choices before youngsters decide what to request for themselves and for other members of the family. The children wait until the last possible moment before composing a letter to the Kings containing their requests. The letters are drafted with painstaking care. Sentences are phrased and rephrased, spelling is checked and corrected, and the final version may be recopied two or three times before it is judged satisfactory.

Urban children who wish to avoid these literary agonies may decide to deliver their requests orally. Many department stores hire people to dress as

◄ *Joseph admits visitors to the stable in* Nativity, *a painting in oil by Italian artist Federico Fiori Barocci (1526-1612).*

A child carefully composes a letter containing a wish list for the Three Kings.

A boy in Santesteban deposits his letter in a mailbox for Olentzero, a traditional gift-bearing character that is a particular favorite in the Basque region of northern Spain.

the Three Kings and listen patiently to the children's wishes. Youngsters who are especially eager for the Kings' attention often stand in line for quite some time and then, as an extra reminder, hand over their letters at the end of the visit.

To avoid the accusation that they are selfish, Spanish youngsters always ask for things for other members of the family as well as for themselves. Parents admonish their children that if they do not behave, the Kings may leave them nothing but a lump of coal. Rarely, if ever, does a real lump of coal actually materialize on Three Kings' morning. But Spanish sweet shops display sugary lumps of candy colored black and shaped like coal as a means to keep mischievous little ones in line.

The story of the Three Kings

The Three Kings have long held a special place in the Spanish Christmas season. The oldest Spanish drama in existence, *Auto de los Reyes Magos,* tells the story of the Kings' search for the Christ child. It is the only example of Spanish medieval liturgical drama that remains in existence today. Unfortunately, only a fragment of 147 verses has been preserved. No exact date is known for the fragment, but authorities place its composition at about 1150.

Children in Carmona, in the province of Andalusia, visit with two of the Three Kings and tell them the gifts they wish for.

The play was presented in the cathedral of Toledo, doubtless over many Christmases, with no costumes or stage settings except a star. Choirboys played all the roles.

The Three Kings appear onstage, first separately and then together, to discuss the mysterious new star in the east and what it might mean. Speaking in rhymed couplets, they decide the star must symbolize the birth of a messiah, and they resolve to visit the child and see which of their gifts he will choose —gold, frankincense, or myrrh. The scene shifts abruptly to Herod's palace, and the fragment breaks off as a worried Herod consults his astrologers to find out what the new star might portend.

The action of the play is simple and naive, which is not surprising. The drama is one of the first to be written in a popular language, rather than in Latin. Still, the characterizations are realistic. The Kings are hesitant at first to follow the star, and Herod is quite believable as he broods over his astrologers' refusal to give him a definitive answer. It is easy to see in the fragment both the playwright's attempt to extract real drama from the story and the origins of the Three Kings' appeal to the Spanish imagination.

*A candy store owner arranges
a tempting display of dulces
to attract shoppers in the
weeks before New Year's and
Three Kings.*

The Feast of the Holy Innocents

Most people are familiar with the rest of the story: the royal trio's arrival at last in Bethlehem and Herod's decision to eliminate the threat of future trouble by sending his soldiers to slay every newborn Jewish boy. Herod's grisly decision is commemorated today by the Roman Catholic Church as the Feast of the Holy Innocents, and December 28 is set aside as a day to honor Herod's victims.

The Feast of the Holy Innocents is still celebrated, and with great enthusiasm, by the people of Spain. But over the centuries, the natural mirth and spontaneity of children has transformed the occasion from a day of mourning to one of gaiety, game-playing, and the playing of practical jokes. Today, December 28 is the Spanish equivalent of April Fool's Day, and April Fool's Day dates back to at least 1582 and maybe to Ancient Rome.

Young men in the Pyrenees build bonfires at the gateways to their towns and from among their number elect a mock mayor, a sort of Spanish Lord of Misrule. This merry official is empowered to assess fines for alleged offenses, and he imposes an absurd law and order by forcing citizens to sweep the streets. Money from the fines is used to pay for the town's festivities.

Spanish youngsters, like those the world over, love to play games. Variations on "hide-and-seek" and "musical chairs," tag games and guessing games, "find

*Suckling pig and other cold meats in a delicatessen
window tempt passersby during the holiday season.*

Throughout the country, friends and neighbors
spend the evening feasting and making merry. Especially among young adults in the cities, merrymaking
does not begin until after midnight, when traffic jams
make it seem like rush hour on a work day.

Residents of the larger cities select whatever entertainment suits their fancy and their pocketbook.
Luxury hotels and restaurants offer entertainment
packages that combine dinner and dancing. Opera
and theater buffs have a variety of performances from
which to choose. Music lovers may go to hear a classical
recital or an ear-splitting rock concert.

In smoky *tavernas*, dancers perform the amazing variety of folk dances to which Spain has given birth: the
butterfly-like *bolero;* the *giraldilla* from Seville; the *fan-
dango* from Huelva; or the *jota* from Aragon. And, of
course, in almost every music hall or nightclub, a
woman in mantilla, high comb, sleeveless bodice, and
wide, flounced skirts stamps and claps her way through
the extraordinary flamenco.

The end of the old year and birth of the new offers
yet another excuse for enjoying a hearty and elaborate
dinner. In many homes, the New Year's Eve meal is
washed down with generous glasses of champagne or
cava and topped off with the traditional holiday
dessert, turrón.

The wealthier Spanish families celebrate the occasion
in truly elaborate fashion. At their banquets, every conceivable delicacy is temptingly displayed. Gentlemen
wear white tie and tails, and the ladies don their most
elegant gowns, accented by precious jewels and the
finest lace.

Pork is a popular favorite as a New Year's Eve entrée.
Perhaps this tradition goes back to the ancient custom
of sacrificing a wild boar in honor of the new year. The
cochinillo (suckling pig) served in Segovia, north of
Madrid, is especially succulent. Since Spain has a lim-
ited supply of both grazing land and cooking fuel, the
Iberians long ago adopted the practice of slaughtering
livestock when an animal is fairly young. The delicate
flavor and crispness of the Segovian cochinillo provide
a memorable culinary experience.

In Andalusia, the provincial capital of Granada produces an extraordinary, pungent, dark-red ham, which

the hidden object" games—all these and more are en-
joyed during the post-Christmas holidays. Charades are
especially popular, and Biblical stories in prose and
verse are acted out with great relish.

On Holy Innocents Day, party-going youngsters
divide themselves into two groups: soldiers and *los
inocentes.* Soldiers write out verses or riddles and pin
them to the backs of los inocentes. The latter have to
figure out the contents by asking a series of yes-or-no
questions.

Welcoming a new year

*T*he next high point in the long wait for the Three
Kings is, of course, New Year's Eve. Spaniards ring
out the old year and welcome the new with a great deal
of gaiety and laughter, much like the rest of the world.
But in the countryside especially, this universal holiday
is observed with a few uniquely Spanish customs.

A family chooses grapes at a market in Valencia, in southeastern Spain. At the stroke of midnight on New Year's Eve, Spaniards eat one grape for each stroke of the clock, to ensure happiness in all twelve months of the new year.

For the same reason, few homemakers in central and southern Spain make their own bread. The donkey cart from the local *panadería* makes daily deliveries of crusty, round loaves every morning. Later in the day, children may be sent to the bakery for another loaf or two for dinner—Spanish people do not like to eat "stale" bread.

One of the best known of the old *churrerías*, or pastry shops, in Madrid is behind the Church of San Ginés, more or less around the corner from the Puerta del Sol. In the days when the Puerta del Sol was famous for its bustling, all-night cafés, the Chocolatería San Ginés often served as the last stop for merrymakers who had passed the night in drinking and socializing.

It is not at all unusual to see people in evening clothes at the churrerías early on New Year's morning. Nor is it uncommon to see jewel-laden ladies

Fireworks light the sky behind a statue of Christopher Columbus in the Plaza de Colón in Madrid on New Year's Eve. The plaza honors Columbus, whose name in Spanish is Cristóbal Colón.

in floor-length gowns escorted to early morning Mass on January 1 by gentlemen in tuxedos. Having welcomed the new year in with revelry, then reverence, most Spaniards spend the rest of the day recovering.

Luck and the fairies

Far to the north of windswept Madrid, in the shadow of the high Pyrenees, ancient customs live on among the fiercely independent Basques and Catalans. On the last night of the old year, fairies, or *hadas,* are supposed to come, bringing good luck in the right hand and bad luck in the left.

Pyreneans open doors to the fairies and even give them their own special room, spotlessly clean and supplied with a meal of bread and wine. The church fathers banned this custom more than 1,500 years ago, but the prohibition seems to have had little effect.

In the morning, the master of the house checks the fairies' room. If there is any bread left over, he breaks it up and distributes it among all the members of the household. It is said that villagers who provide liberally for the hadas are rewarded in the new year with large harvests and increased flocks.

This custom seems related to the Bacchanalia of ancient Rome—the revels held in honor of the god of wine and merrymaking. The Romans believed that the dead returned to their homes for these riotous celebrations and were, therefore, careful to prepare for the return of the departed. The Romans spread tables for the family ghosts and even went so far as to leave dice out so that the ghosts could have something to amuse themselves with while the living feasted and danced.

In the Basque region, a fairly recent custom draws thousands of participants. In the mid-1900's, Basques began welcoming in the new year by climbing a mountain near their village. After a rousing New Year's Eve celebration, townspeople and visitors start a two-to-three-hour journey up the mountain. The ascent has come to symbolize letting go of the past year. Reaching the peak—ideally before sunrise—symbolizes looking to what lies ahead. The symbolism has a practical side, too. The vigorous hike is a healthy way of working off any remaining effects from the midnight celebration. It also gives the revelers another occasion to uncork a bottle of cava, share some turrón, join their neighbors in song, and set off some fireworks.

In many places within the Basque region, a character called Olentzero sits in the corner of the village tavern on New Year's Eve with a cauldron on his head and a scythe in his hand. After Olentzero has been properly chastised for drinking too much, the young men of the village take him outside and carry him from house to house, singing as they go. The wassailing, or toasting, of fruit trees to ensure a good harvest is another New Year's task performed by young men in this region of Spain.

The days between Christmas and January 6 are a delightful, fascinating blend of Christian beliefs and secular customs in Spain. Even Papa Noel may have made a Christmas Day or Christmas Eve appearance at the homes of some families. But his hold on the hearts and minds of Spanish youngsters hardly equals that of the beloved royal figures from the east. As January 6 approaches, the children's excitement rises to a fever pitch.

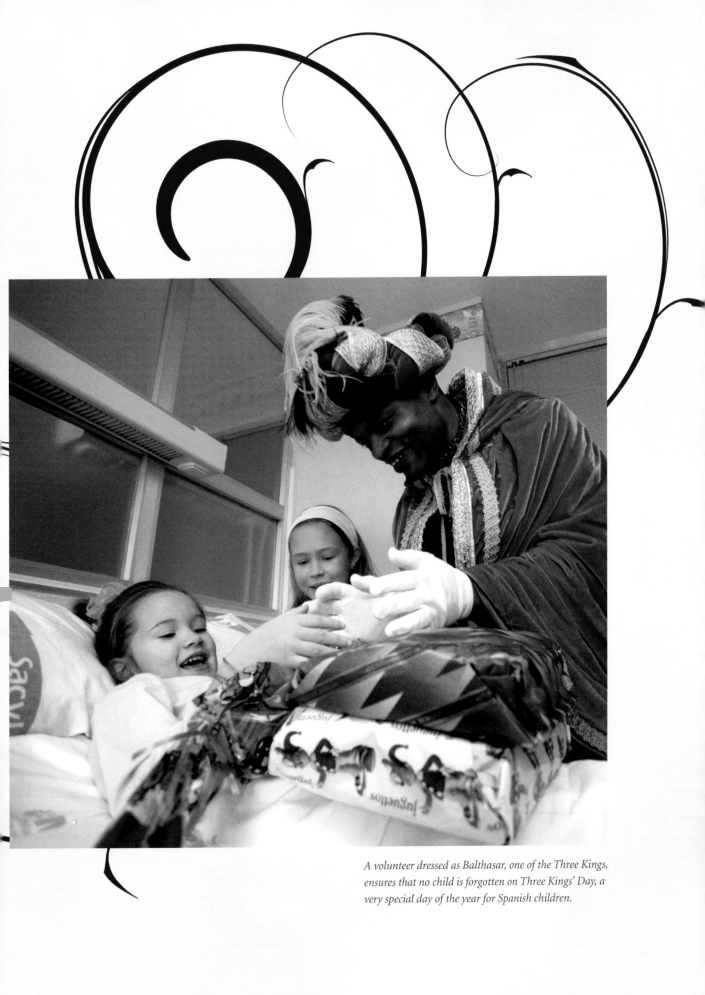

A volunteer dressed as Balthasar, one of the Three Kings, ensures that no child is forgotten on Three Kings' Day, a very special day of the year for Spanish children.

Feast of the Epiphany

*S*panish tradition holds that the Three Kings (or Magi) from the East set out for Spain each year on January 5, the eve of the Epiphany, to pay homage to the infant Christ. They don their finest robes, mount their horses, camels, or donkeys, and leave with an elaborate retinue of pack animals and servants.

In the past, it was customary to go out to meet the Magi on Three Kings' Eve. Young and old alike would march to the edge of town or to the city gates carrying cakes for the Kings, as well as a selection of straw, carrots, oats, and assorted other foods for the Kings' animals and servants.

The children trudged along with lamps mounted on poles and torches held aloft so that the Three Kings could find their way more easily. There was, of course, a certain amount of self-interest in this act of kindness. It was well known that the Kings were bearing gifts, not only for the Holy Infant, but for every child in Spain.

Parents in the procession carried rattles and bells to provide a warm-hearted welcome for the great caravan. They blew horns and beat on pots and pans with spoons and sticks. Someone in the group usually brought along a ladder. Every once in a while the lookout would stop, set up his ladder, and peer into the night to see if he could locate *los Reyes Magos*.

These elaborate and well-intentioned efforts, however, never seemed to succeed. No matter how sharp the lookout, the Kings always seemed to pass by the town on another road. One would think they would have seen the lights or heard the noise made by the welcoming committee. But somehow the two groups always seemed to miss each other.

There was nothing for the youngsters to do but throw away the straw, eat the cakes and goodies themselves, and return home, weary and disappointed. But then the parents would suggest that the Three Kings had probably assembled at the great Nacimiento in the village church. It sometimes took some talking to

A child prepares for Three Kings' Day, leaving straw, food, and water for the royal visitors' animals and a pair of her shoes to be filled with gifts by the Kings themselves.

◀ *The Three Kings worship the Christ child in a fresco (wall painting) by Ferrer Bassa (1290?–1348) in the Chapel of Sant Miguel, Monastery of Pedralbes, Barcelona.*

persuade sleepy little ones to check at the church before going to bed. But as is usually the case, the parents won out.

In the radiant candlelight illuminating the communal Nacimiento, the villagers would discover Melchior, Gaspar, and Balthasar kneeling reverently before the Christ child, presenting their gifts of gold, frankincense, and myrrh. The entire community would join in singing the traditional Epiphany carol, "This Morn I Met the Train of the Kings." (Strictly speaking, of course, this claim was not accurate.)

The Church and the Epiphany

*I*t appears that the Roman Catholic Church in Spain played a significant role in assigning to the Feast of the Epiphany the prominence it now enjoys. In Spain during the 300's, a long fast marked the season of Advent, which in those times ended on January 6. A document from the council of Saragossa, which dates from around 380, decreed a 21-day fast, from December 17 to January 6. During this time, the faithful were not supposed to dance or make merry, but were instead to devote themselves to prayer and worship. Certain prelates even refused to perform the marriage rites during this period. Needless to say, the feast that marked the end of Advent was celebrated with gusto.

The word *epiphany* comes from a Greek word meaning "manifestation" or "revelation." In ancient times, the Feast of the Epiphany commemorated Christ's Nativity, which was assumed to have taken place on January 6. The day was also associated with the baptism of Jesus, an event that marked the beginning of Christ's ministry on Earth and revealed him to be the Son of God.

After December 25 was widely accepted as Christ's actual birthday, the Feast of the Epiphany became associated with the arrival of the Magi in Bethlehem, since they were the first to whom the Messiah was revealed through the miraculous appearance of the Christmas star. To this day, January 6, Three Kings' Day, is also known as "little Christmas" or "old Christmas" in certain parts of Spain.

Three Kings' eve

*S*paniards still go out to meet the Three Kings on the evening of January 5. But in larger towns and cities, at least, their efforts are rewarded by a *cabalgata,* a festive and showy parade that brings the Kings to town in grand fashion.

At no time during the Christmas holidays is the Spanish love of color and pageantry more readily apparent than on Epiphany Eve. Youngsters and their parents line the streets to welcome the royal visitors and their entourage. The stars of the cabalgata appear in full regalia. Crowned heads glisten and gleam with artificial gems. The Kings' long, trailing robes, adorned with fanciful embroidery, amaze and delight the onlookers.

The Magi may sweep past on flower-bedecked floats, waving to their admirers and tossing candy and little treats to wide-eyed youngsters. Balthazar is the children's favorite; it is he who most commonly distributes turrón and other goodies.

Sometimes the Kings ride live animals into town. Balthasar usually arrives astride a donkey. The other Kings may be mounted on horseback or, in the bigger parades, they may even sway through town upon camels.

It would be most unseemly for the Kings to travel alone. The fancier and more elaborate their entourage, the better, from satin-clad pages and court jesters to every imaginable kind of servant. Marching bands may precede the royal trio, clearing a path and, with their booming bass drums, setting the pace for the cabalgata. Jugglers, clowns, stilt-walkers, and mummers in fanciful costumes also join in the festivities.

Cabalgatas are held in most of the larger towns and cities on the evening of January 5. The larger the community, the bigger and more colorful the parade. Madrid, Barcelona, Palma de Mallorca, Málaga, Lérida, and Seville put on wonder-filled, elaborate cabalgatas.

The eagerly awaited Three Kings wave to cheering crowds as they arrive on a float in a parade in Barcelona.

Holiday excitement seems to reach a peak on the eve of Three Kings' Day. Many stores stay open until midnight to accommodate last-minute shoppers. There is probably no other night in the year on which Spanish parents have a more difficult time persuading their children to go to bed—or on which children find it harder to drift off to sleep.

Gifts from the Kings

Just before retiring, every member of the family puts out a pair of shoes, with full confidence that during the night the Kings will come to fill the shoes with presents and treats. Children, parents, and grandparents alike participate in this tradition. In the long rows

A flock of geese sporting Christmas ornaments lead an Epiphany parade in Madrid.

of apartment buildings and condominium complexes in which the majority of urban Spaniards live, shoes are placed outside on the balconies. They may also be put at the window, the door, or near the fireplace.

In most families, parents will leave out three dishes of food for the Kings and perhaps three glasses of wine as well. The animals are not forgotten, either. The children usually stuff their shoes with straw for the royal camels, or they will leave out oats, barley, carrots or other delicacies, depending on the kind of transportation they imagine the gift bringers are riding.

Some families possess two different sets of Kings for the family Nacimiento. One set shows the trio astride camels. It is put in place on Christmas Eve and left there until January 5, to show that the Kings are en route to Bethlehem. On the Eve of the Epiphany, a new set of Kings replaces the first after the children have gone to sleep. This one shows the trio kneeling devotedly before the crib, present-

ing their gifts—proof that the Kings have arrived at the manger and have visited the household during the night. In homes with only one set of Kings, parents simply move the figures closer to the crib on the night of January 5.

The children can barely contain their excitement the morning of January 6. They get up at the crack of dawn to inspect their shoes and see what the Kings have brought for them. The straw, of course, has disappeared, as has the food left out for the Magi. The children's shoes are stuffed with candy and other treats and surrounded with presents. So, in fact, are the shoes put out by the grown-up members of the family.

In many parts of Spain, generous members of the community will visit the homes of the poor on the night of January 5. They empty shoes of straw and replace it with fruit, nuts, turrón, and other treats. On January 6, some Spaniards dress up as the Three Kings and deliver gifts to children in hospitals and orphanages.

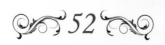

A traditional Epiphany parade, held the evening before Three Kings' Day, often includes marching bands.

The history of the Kings

The Three Kings have long appealed to the Spanish imagination and, in fact, to Christendom at large. However, the role they play in the celebration of Christmas is remarkable when one considers that the only biblical mention of them is a brief account in the Gospel of St. Matthew. Matthew's account does not supply their names, tell us where they came from, or, for that matter, even specify how many there were.

Over the years after Matthew penned his account, the Magi began to take on a life of their own. Each acquired a name, a background, a unique personality. Eventually, they were even given their own feast day.

There is a certain magic and mysterious appeal in Matthew's account of the Magi. They were apparently the only ones to whom the Christmas star appeared. It guided them safely to the manger in Bethlehem, and divine intervention kept the Kings from revealing Christ's birthplace to the wicked Herod.

Clearly, people wanted to believe in the story of the Three Kings. Their presence at the manger adds a symbolic touch to the scene. At one end of the scale, humble shepherds (mentioned in St. Luke's Nativity account) kneel in adoration of the newborn Savior. At the other end, the royal visitors submit their temporal power to the divine authority of the Christ child.

In Matthew's account, the Three Kings were not kings at all. The Latin word *magi* in the early scriptures refers specifically to astrologer-priests of Persia (now called Iran). In time, embellishers added the meaning of wisemen/philosophers. It was not until the end of the 500's that the words "magi" and "kings" began to be used interchangeably to refer to Matthew's star-guided visitors. The new name was based on the work of the early Christian writer Tertullian (160?-225), who linked the travelers to two Old Testament prophecies that kings bearing gifts would come to Israel.

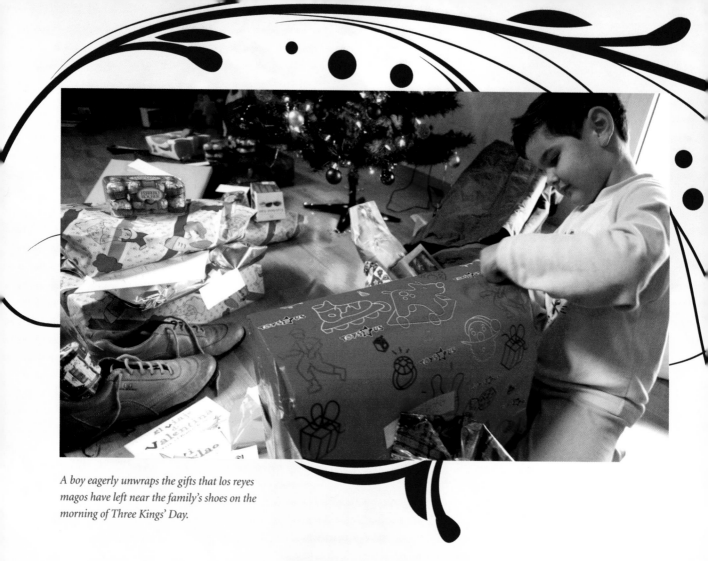

A boy eagerly unwraps the gifts that los reyes magos have left near the family's shoes on the morning of Three Kings' Day.

The popular imagination was stirred as much by the nature of the regal gifts as it was by speculation on the identity of the bearers. Gold, of course, is a precious metal; frankincense and myrrh—aromatic resins—were highly valued as incense. Later the gifts acquired symbolic meaning as well. Gold was understood to stand for the virtue of love and also to symbolize Christ as the king of the world. Frankincense, a very sweet spice, became identified with prayer or with Christ as the king of heaven. Myrrh, which comes from the bark of a thorny African tree, came to represent suffering and the sacrifice that Christ made on the cross.

One church scholar, Jacobus de Voragine, had a more practical interpretation of the Magi's gifts: the gold was intended to relieve the Holy Family's poverty; frankincense would be useful in disguising objectionable stable smells; and myrrh could be used as an antidote for vermin.

Matthew's mention of three gifts was ultimately responsible for a papal decree that the Magi were three in number. Early church art portrays two or four gift bearers. St. Augustine preferred the number 12, symbolic of the 12 apostles and the 12 tribes of Israel.

By the 700's, the oldest of the three Magi was called Melchior. Gaspar was a young man, and Balthasar was often pictured as a black man, one who had traveled from faraway Ethiopia.

At some point in the growth of the Three Kings legend, the figures passed into Spanish folklore and became responsible for distributing gifts to worthy children. In other countries, this task fell to Santa Claus, St. Nicholas, Befana (in Italy), or even the Christ child himself. But in Spain, it is the Kings who are the source of youngsters' delight at Christmastime.

Spanish presents are not exchanged from one person to another. The Kings give them all. On January 6, once the children have opened their gifts at home, the family most likely will go to visit relatives to see what the Kings may have left for them there. Visitors also will bring along gifts that the Kings have left at their house for cousins, aunts, uncles, and other members of the extended family.

Vendors display their roscón, a traditional Kings' Day treat with a prize hidden inside. The prize ensures good luck during the coming year for the person who finds it.

Hidden luck in the roscón

The traditional Kings' Day treat is *roscón*, a kind of fruitcake with a tiny, inexpensive toy hidden inside. Roscón is delicious and much loved. It is served either plain or topped with luscious whipped cream. On Three Kings' Day, Spaniards will eat as much roscón as possible and as often as possible: at breakfast, lunch, and in the afternoon as a snack.

Anyone who discovers the toy in his or her piece of roscón is destined to enjoy good luck in the coming year. Should a parent be served the trinket, the mother or father will most likely try to sneak it back into a piece of roscón that is destined for one of the children. Little ones get a huge amount of pleasure from guessing who will find the toy, but especially from discovering it themselves.

Three Kings' Day brings the Spanish Christmas holidays to a happy conclusion. The lilting strains of the traditional villancicos seem to fade with the last rays of the sun, not to be heard again for another year. The family Nacimiento is packed away lovingly with the other holiday decorations. Families who put up Christmas trees know that the time has come to take them down. Children who had so much trouble getting to sleep the night before go to bed willingly on Three Kings' Day. The excitement is over at last, and they have much to dream about.

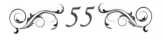

The Christmas Story in Spanish Art

Through the centuries, Spanish artists have portrayed the Christmas story in paintings, frescoes, sculptures, wood carvings, and many other mediums. Their exquisite works decorate cathedrals, monasteries, and museums throughout the country.

No aspect of the Christmas story has escaped the attention of Spanish artists—from the angel Gabriel's surprise visit announcing to Mary that she is to become the mother of God to the Holy Family's flight into Egypt to protect their newborn son from Herod's legions. Outstanding portrayals of the Nativity by traditional artists include works by the painters El Greco (1541?–1614) and Diego Velázquez (1599–1660) and the sculptures of the Transparente, a Baroque altarpiece, in the Toledo Cathedral. Barcelona's Sagrada Familia, the church designed by Spanish architect Antonio Gaudí (1852–1926), is a modern tribute to the Holy Family.

On a different, but no less important, scale, the story of the Nativity has fired the imaginations of generations of Spanish folk artists. The creation of Nacimiento scenes for family, village, school, and church has been a universal pre-Christmas activity in Spain for centuries, and it is only natural that this popular folk art has reached a high level of development.

Spanish Nacimiento figures have been fashioned from every conceivable material: wood, clay, wax, plaster, straw, even cardboard. Often there are several belenistas involved in the creation of the elaborate Nacimientos produced by the clubs and organizations devoted to building and displaying the crèches, or Bethlehems. A skilled woodworker might transform a piece of scrap pine into a figure of Balthasar, the Ethiopian King. A local housepainter-turned-artisan might color in the hands and face of the Magi figure, then turn it over to a seamstress or tailor to be fitted for royal robes. Yet another set of skilled fingers might decorate the robes with rich embroidery, then send the king to a metalsmith or jeweler to be crowned.

A special museum has been created to preserve a huge Nacimiento created by the popular sculptor Francisco Salzillo (1707–1781). The Museo Salzillo (Salzillo Museum) is housed in a former chapel in Murcia, 30 miles (48 kilometers) north of Cartagena, near the southeast coast. Salzillo's Nacimiento includes 372 animal figures and 184 little figures of peasants. All sculpted in terra cotta and hand painted, they possess an amazing vitality.

Every Spanish town and village seems to have one or two families who are particularly adept at the creation of Nacimiento figures. But the Salzillo family must

Grecian columns adorn a Nacimiento displayed among more than 1,500 other Nativity scenes at the Museo Salzillo in Murcia.

◀ *A Nativity scene depicted in exquisite detail forms part of the fantastic façade of Gaudí's church of the Sagrada Familia in Barcelona.*

The Madonna and Child have been favorite subjects for Spanish artists throughout the ages.

hold the record for mass production. Francisco, with the help of his sister and brothers, is said to have carved or sculpted about 4,000 figures in his lifetime.

Immortalizing Madonna and Child

The theme of the Madonna and Child has been interpreted by countless Spanish artists since the beginning of the Christian era. The *polychrome* (multicolored) wooden sculptures depicted top and center at left display two stern examples from the period of Romanesque art (1000-1300) and a far more approachable representation (bottom) dating from the Renaissance (1300-1600).

The top figure is from the early 1100's. Few free-standing sculptures were created during this period. The Romanesque was essentially an architectural style, and most sculpture was executed in relief as simple adornment, subordinate to the building as a whole. This example is intended to be viewed, or worshiped, from the front only, the sides being originally hidden in an architectural niche.

Romanesque sculptors were preoccupied with evoking the spiritual quality of a subject, rather than capturing a three-dimensional representation. The artist has chosen to emphasize the Madonna's eyes, considered to be windows to the soul. The statue is frozen in a timeless universe of the spirit, far removed from our own sensual world. The piece has a primitive vitality that is typically Catalan. The approach is direct, forceful, unpretentious —clearly the product of a folk artist. A strong Byzantine influence can also be seen in the exuberant use of color and very formal approach to the Christ child. He is not a newborn, but rather a miniature adult, regal in bearing, raising his arm in blessing.

The middle statue is another example from the same period. It has the static, other-world quality characteristic of the Romanesque, but the emphasis is different. Here the Madonna and Child are monarchs, the king and queen of heaven. Both figures are crowned, and they are seated on a throne. This is a departure from the more provincial treatment of the Catalan Mother and Child. Still, the movement in the middle piece is away from the worldly. It is meant to excite our spiritual nature, to redirect our gaze toward heaven. The eyes are even more pronounced, and both figures seem frozen in eternity. The Byzantine influence is still strong, especially in the stripes decorating the throne.

Renaissance artists took a more humanistic approach in their work. The third example dates from the mid-1500's. The flat, two-dimensional quality of the Romanesque has been discarded. The piece is fluid, richly textured, and fully realistic. The Christ child is a rosy-cheeked baby, not a little adult. The Madonna is warm, sweet, maternal—very human, definitely approachable. Except for the Madonna's costume, this mother and child might be found in our own century.

Romanesque artists would never have dreamed of picturing Christ as a naked baby. But Renaissance artists characteristically celebrated the human body for itself. The emphasis here is on Christ's humanity. The way to salvation, by Renaissance times, lay in full participation in the life of this world, not in stony contemplation of the next.

The Nativity through the ages

The 1600's produced numerous artistic interpretations of the events of the Nativity, including masterworks by three of Spain's greatest artists: Juan Martínez Montañés (1568-1649), El Greco, and Diego Rodríguez de Silva y Velázquez.

Montañés is generally recognized as Spain's greatest sculptor in wood. Born in 1568, he passed the examinations for master sculptor at the age of 20. During his long life, he produced a vast quantity of work, almost all devoted to religious subjects.

Christ on the Cross, commissioned in 1603 by the Archdeacon Vázquez de Leca, established Montañés's reputation as a sculptor. It is considered the most perfect Spanish example of this demanding subject. The happier theme of the Nativity is best represented by the artist's *Adoration of the Shepherds.*

Like most of Montañés's statues, the *Adoration* is gilded and painted in oil, probably by the artist's friend Francisco Pacheco. It measures 47 inches (119 centimeters) by 79 inches (201 centimeters) and is crafted with loving attention to detail. A curious ox and donkey, for example, poke their heads out from their stall to see what is disturbing the stable's customary quiet. Wisps of straw extend from the donkey's mouth, its pleasure in its evening snack forever captured in wood. Completed between 1610 and 1613, the *Adoration of the Shepherds* can be seen today at the Monastery of San Isidro del Campo in Santiponce.

Domenikos Theotokopoulos, called El Greco (The Greek) by admirers in his adopted country, Spain, occupies a unique niche in the history of art. He was born in Crete and studied in Venice, but the Spaniards claimed him as their own. His work, however, transcends national borders and can only be described as distinctively his own.

El Greco had no contemporary biographers, and none of his diaries or theoretical writings has ever been found. In 1977, however, Professor of Art History Fernando Marías of the Universidad Autónoma de Madrid and his colleague Professor Agustín Bustamante Garcia discovered an edition of Vitruvius's *On Architecture* from the 1500's. The work contained notes in El Greco's distinctive, Mediterranean mix of Italian, Spanish, and Greek. The artist wrote that the ladies of Toledo who wore high-heeled shoes *(chapines)* knew more about beauty than artists of the time who utilized mathematical formulas to meet Renaissance standards of perspective and proportion.

El Greco was familiar with the works of the Italian Renaissance, having lived in Italy for almost 20 years in the 1560's and 1570's. During his stay, he became familiar with the Venetian style of painting known as mannerism, which is marked by long, graceful lines, elongated and abstract forms, and metallic colors accented with white highlights. The influence of this approach to painting is readily apparent in his later work.

El Greco moved to Toledo, Spain, in 1577, and it was in Spain that he created his greatest paintings. Something in the country's religious atmosphere seems to have drawn forth and nourished his inborn mysticism. "The light of day clouds the inner light," he once told a friend who found him shut up in his studio, with shutters drawn, on a beautiful summer day.

If the search for inner light was the driving force of El Greco's personality, the bold, imaginative use of color and light also characterized his greatest paintings. Nowhere is this more apparent than in his magnificent *Adoration of the Shepherds* (see page 60)—the same subject that inspired the sculptor Montañés.

El Greco's painting is one of the most transcendent interpretations of the Nativity ever put on canvas. The Christ child at the heart of the picture is the primary source of light, radiating with an intensity that throws every other figure in the composition into sharp relief. The swirling ring of cherubs above, the elongated figures of the shepherds—all are transfigured by the Light of the World.

El Greco used to fashion small figures in wax, then arrange and rearrange them in groups, like a Spanish child playing with the family Nacimiento. In the *Adoration of the Shepherds,* the composition perfectly

El Greco's Adoration of the
Shepherds *(1614) was the last
painting the artist produced.*

expresses El Greco's transcendent theme. The worshipers are arranged in a lyrical upward spiral, with
the Christ child at the center. The shepherd stand-
ing on the right seems about to be transported into
heaven. The angels above are buoyed by the Baby's
spiritual energy.

The *Adoration* was the last painting El Greco produced. It was intended to hang above his tomb in
the church of Santo Domingo el Antiguo in Toledo,
where he had painted his earliest works in Spain. In

1619, five years after El Greco's death, his son, Jorge
Manuel Theotokopoulos, moved the family vault to
San Torcuato in Toledo. The church was destroyed
in the 19th century, and the artist's tomb vanished
with it. Fortunately, the *Adoration of the Shepherds*
still hangs today in the church of Toledo's cloistered
Convent of Santo Domingo el Antiguo.

Velázquez's *Adoration of the Magi* (see page 61)
is another work from the 1600's, painted approximately five years after El Greco completed the

*Velázquez, a court painter, used his
wife and child as models for his work*
Adoration of the Magi *(1619).*

Adoration of the Shepherds. A comparison of the
two is revealing.

Velázquez was for most of his career a successful
court painter, interested primarily in portraits and
secular themes. So it is natural that when he
turned to the Nativity, the subjects he chose were
royal visitors, not humble shepherds. Velázquez,
like El Greco, knew the importance of light and
shadow. But in Velázquez's painting, the figures are
thrown into relief by the last rays of a setting sun,
not illuminated by the Christ child's inner light.

The *Adoration of the Magi* is a static composition, painted early in the artist's career (1619).
Veláz-quez's wife and baby served as the models
for Madonna and Child; he included his teacher,
Pacheco, in the role of the grey-bearded king.
Though the Magi exhibit reverent devotion,
no one is about to rise into heaven. (El Greco's
masterpiece, on the other hand, is transcendent
and ecstatic.)

Construction of Gaudí's extravagant Sagrada Familia, begun in the 1880's, continues today. Each of the façades depicts details from the life of Christ.

Architectural treasures

The Transparente—an enormous baroque altarpiece in Toledo's Gothic cathedral—is unsurpassed in theatricality, even in a century of extraordinarily dramatic architecture. Created by Spanish architect and sculptor Narcisco Tóme (1690-1742) between 1721 and 1732, the work is an ornate confection of clouds, columns, saints, and angels in both low and high relief. In the central vaulted niche rests a skillfully mounted Madonna and Child executed in marble, jasper, and bronze. The Transparente is illuminated by an aperture in the roof. The effect produced by the light falling upon the altarpiece is nothing short of breathtaking.

Barcelona's Templo Expiatorio de la Sagrada Familia is a modern-day tribute to the Holy Family. It has been variously described as "early psychedelic," "the most extravagant fancy ever conceived in ecclesiastical architecture," "glorious," "bizarre," "a work of genius," and "Gaudí's folly." Today it is used to symbolize this great city.

The building is the masterwork of Antonio Gaudí, whose death—he was run over by a tram in 1926—was as surrealistic as his distinctive architectural style. Begun in the 1880's, the Sagrada Familia has still not been completed, and construction of the building continues today. When and how it is completed will depend to a great extent on the availability of donations.

The main porch is topped by a gigantic stone Christmas tree, painted a climactic green. Four enormously tall fluted pinnacles taper oddly to the sky, each capped by a sort of giant sunburst bordered by toy balloons. Gaudí's plan for the church calls for eight more of these spires, of which an additional four have been completed.

It was Gaudí's desire to re-create Gothic art, but in a context inspired by the rich flowering of Catalan art at the turn of the century. The artist worked more as a sculptor than as an architect. He changed his ideas often as the work went on, molding huge masses of material with the freedom and exuberance of a child building a sand castle.

The Sagrada Familia's existing three façades, which portray events connected with the birth and life of Christ, seem literally to grow from the pavement. Stone vines climb upward to provide niches for statues of Biblical characters. What in a regular church would be a pillar becomes a tree in Gaudí's structure. The artist's love of nature is everywhere apparent, right down to the families of stone chickens scratching realistically on either side of the main entrance. To Gaudí, religion encompassed all living things.

Each generation of Spanish artists and artisans interprets the Christmas story in its own unique fashion. There is no way to predict, of course, when the next El Greco or Gaudí will emerge. We can only watch, with pleasure, as the Christmas story continues to unfold in Spanish art.

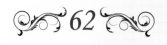

A Spanish Christmas Vocabulary

Belenes: "Bethlehems," or Nativity scenes.

Belenista: A person who makes Nativity scenes.

Besugo al horno: Baked sea bream, the traditional fish course of the Spanish Christmas meal.

Cabalgata: The parade held in towns and cities on the evening of January 5 to welcome the Three Kings.

Cava: A sparkling wine produced in Catalonia and often served on Christmas Eve.

Churros: The Spanish equivalent of doughnuts, often purchased from street vendors or at a café.

Danza de los Seises: The Dance of the Sixes; performed by choirboys in traditional costume before the altar of the Seville cathedral on December 8 to usher in the holidays.

El Gordo: A lottery held annually throughout Spain on December 22.

Feliz Navidad: Merry Christmas.

Los Inocentes: The Jewish male babies slaughtered by Herod's soldiers, commemorated by a feast on December 28.

Los Reyes Magos: The Three Kings.

Mantecados: Traditional Spanish cookies made with almonds.

Mazapán: Marzipan, a candy widely eaten at Christmastime.

Misa del Gallo: Christmas Eve midnight Mass (literally, "Mass of the cock's crow").

Nacimiento: The crèche, or Nativity scene, that is found in almost every Spanish home at Christmastime.

Navidad: Christmas.

Nochebuena: Christmas Eve (literally, the "good night").

Papa Noel: Santa Claus.

Pavo: Turkey, the main course of the traditional Spanish Christmas meal.

Paz en la Tierra a los Hombres de Buena Voluntad: Peace on Earth to People of Good Will.

Próspero año nuevo: Happy New Year.

Roscón de Reyes: The traditional treat for Three Kings' Day, a fruitcake with an inexpensive toy hidden inside.

Tió de Nadal: Yule log.

Tuna: A lively band of university students in traditional dress who sing and play music.

Turrón: A kind of nougat made of toasted almonds, sugar, honey, and eggs, eaten universally during the Christmas holidays.

Villancicos: Traditional Spanish Christmas carols.

Yemas: Confection made of egg yolks, sugar, and lemon eaten throughout the Christmas season.

Zambomba: A hollow, cylindrical folk instrument that produces a rhythmic whine when a stick is moved up and down through a skin stretched over the top; widely used to accompany Christmas carols.

Spanish Treats

Medias Lunas de Nueces
(nut crescents)

  1⅔ cups flour
  ½ lb. unsalted butter
  1 cup ground walnuts
  1 tsp. vanilla
  ½ cup confectioners' sugar
  pinch of salt

Mix the flour and butter together until they form crumbs. Add walnuts, vanilla, salt, and sugar and mix well. If necessary, chill dough about ½ hour or until dough is workable. Preheat oven to 375 °F. Cut dough into walnut-size pieces and roll each piece to about 3 inches in length. Shape each piece into a crescent by pulling it into a semicircle.

Place crescents ½-inch apart on a baking sheet. Bake for 12 to 15 minutes until lightly browned. Dust with confectioners' sugar while warm. Yield: About 20 crescents.

Mantecados
(traditional Spanish crumble cakes)

  2 eggs
  1 lemon
  1 cup vegetable shortening
  ½ cup vegetable oil
  ¾ cup sugar
  1 tsp. anise extract (or 1 shotglass
    anise-flavored liqueur)
  ¼ tsp. ground cinnamon
  3½ cups flour, sifted
  ¼ tsp. baking soda
  dash of salt

Separate egg yolks from egg whites. Use a fork to beat egg whites. Set aside. Grate lemon peel, making sure not to grate the white pith; set aside. Squeeze 2 tsp. juice; set aside.

Preheat oven to 325 °F. In a large bowl, whip the vegetable shortening with an electric mixer. Add the oil. When well blended, add the sugar; mix until smooth. Add egg yolks, lemon peel, lemon juice, anise extract (or liqueur), and cinnamon. Mix well.

Add flour and baking soda to mixture, one cup at a time. Mix well. At the end, the dough will have the texture of wet crumbs.

Using a rounded tablespoon, scoop out dough. Roll between your hands to form a ball. Place balls on ungreased, nonstick cookie sheet. Lightly press down on each ball to flatten slightly. Brush with beaten egg white. Bake cookies until light brown—about 15 to 20 minutes. Cool in pan 2 to 3 minutes, then gently remove to wire rack (cookies will be fragile). Yield: 2½ dozen.

Pastel de Navidad
(Christmas nut cups)

  Pastry sufficient for 1 pie shell

  5 eggs
  ⅔ cup sugar
  5 Tbsp. butter, melted
  pinch of salt
  1 tsp. vanilla
  1 cup chopped walnuts
  ⅔ cup raisins

Preheat oven to 375 °F. Roll pastry thin and cut into 4-inch circles. Fit each round into muffin cup and press in gently. Beat eggs until they are light; add sugar and mix well. Add butter, salt, and vanilla; mix well. Combine walnuts and raisins and fill each cup ½ full. Add egg mixture to fill each cup three-quarters. Bake filled cups 20 to 25 minutes. Yield: 8 to 12 nut cups.

Compota de Manzanas
(apple compote)

6 tart apples, cored and quartered
6 Tbsp. sugar
1 cinnamon stick
1 cup water

Combine sugar, cinnamon stick, and water in a saucepan and simmer for 5 minutes. Cut apple quarters in half, add to saucepan, and cook gently until tender, about 15 to 20 minutes. Remove apples to serving bowl. Simmer syrup 10 minutes and strain over apples. Serve cold. Yield: 6 servings.

Chocolate a la Española
(Spanish-style hot chocolate)

½ lb. sweet baker's chocolate
1 quart milk (or ½ milk, ½ water)
2 tsp. cornstarch

Break chocolate into small pieces. Place in saucepan with liquid. Heat slowly, stirring with a whisk, until just before the boiling point. Dissolve cornstarch in a few tablespoons of cold water. Add dissolved cornstarch to chocolate mixture and stir constantly until the liquid thickens. Serve hot in warmed cups. Yield: 6 small or 4 large servings.

Almendrados
(almond cookies)

2 cups blanched almonds, finely chopped
2 egg whites, room temperature
1 cup sifted confectioners' sugar
1 tsp. vanilla

Preheat oven to 325 °F. Lightly toast almonds; set aside. Beat egg whites until stiff but not dry. Gradually add sugar, beating constantly. After sugar is added, beat 5 to 8 minutes. Fold in almonds and vanilla. Place by spoonfuls or shape into rings on greased cookie sheet. Bake 17 to 20 minutes or until cookies just begin to brown. Yield: About 3 dozen.

Flan
(caramel custard)

Caramelized sugar:
10 Tbsp. sugar
5 tsp. water

Heat sugar and water in small skillet over medium-high heat, stirring constantly, until sugar is golden. Remove from heat and pour into 6 ovenproof custard cups.

Custard:
3 eggs
3 egg yolks
¼ tsp. grated lemon rind
6 Tbsp. sugar
2½ cups milk

Beat eggs and egg yolks together lightly with a wire whisk. Add lemon rind, sugar, and milk. Pour into the caramelized cups and place cups in pan of hot water. Cook on top of stove over medium heat 1 hour. Preheat oven to 350 °F. Cook flan 25 minutes or until knife inserted in center comes out clean. Remove from water and cool, then refrigerate. To serve, loosen sides of custard with knife and invert onto dessert dishes. Yield: 6 servings.

Compota de Peras
(pear compote)

2 lbs. pears
½ lb. sugar
2 cups water
4 oz. red wine
1 cinnamon stick (3 inches)
grated zest of ½ lemon

Peel and core the pears. Place in pot with remaining ingredients and bring to a boil. Cook 10 to 15 minutes, until the pears are very soft but still hold their shape. Serve warm or at room temperature with some of the cooking syrup. Yield: 4 to 6 servings.

Mazapán
(marzipan)

3 cups whole almonds, blanched and ground
2 cups sugar
1 cup water
2 egg whites, lightly beaten
3 to 4 Tbsp. confectioners' sugar
1 tsp. vanilla

In a saucepan, heat water and sugar until sugar dissolves and mixture comes to a boil. Let it boil steadily without stirring until the temperature reaches 230 °F to 234 °F on a candy thermometer. Remove from heat and beat until mixture turns slightly cloudy. Stir in ground almonds, egg whites, and vanilla. Cook over gentle heat for 2 to 3 minutes or until mixture pulls away from sides of pan. Turn mixture onto a surface that has been sprinkled with some of the confectioners' sugar. Knead the mixture until smooth, working in the rest of the confectioners' sugar. Pull off pieces and roll into balls or olive-shaped pieces. Wrap in foil or wax paper and store in airtight container.

Churros
(fried pastry)

1 cup water
½ cup unsalted butter
¼ tsp. salt
1 cup all-purpose flour
4 large eggs
oil for deep frying
confectioners' sugar

In a heavy saucepan, bring water, butter, and salt to full boil. Remove from heat and immediately add the flour all at once, stirring vigorously until the mixture leaves the sides of the pan and forms a ball. Turn mixture into the bowl of an electric mixer. On medium speed, add one egg at a time, beating only until egg is incorporated before adding the next. After adding the last egg, beat for 1 minute more.

If using a pastry bag, fit it with a ½-inch open star tip. (A cookie press can also be used. It should have a star tip.) Pipe out 5- to 6-inch lengths of dough into 2 to 3 inches of oil heated to 375 °F. Fry, turning occasionally, for 3 to 5 minutes or until golden brown. Drain well and sprinkle with sugar.

Carbón Dulce
(lump of coal candy)

½ cup water
2 cups granulated sugar
¾ cup light corn syrup
1 tsp. anise extract
½ tsp. black paste food color
1 tsp. baking soda

Line an 8-inch square baking pan with foil, extending edges over the sides of pan. Lightly grease foil with butter or baking spray.

Combine water, sugar, and corn syrup in a non-stick, 2-quart saucepan. Heat on medium-low, stirring until mixture comes to a boil and sugar is dissolved. Clip a candy thermometer to side of pan (do not let it touch bottom of pan). Cook about 15 minutes without stirring, until thermometer registers 290 °F. Immediately remove from heat. Stir in anise extract, food coloring, and baking soda. Mix well. Pour mixture into prepared baking pan. Cool completely on wire rack.

Lift candy out of pan using foil. Place on cutting board and cover with a sheet of heavy-duty foil. Use a kitchen mallet to break into pieces the size of lumps of coal. Store in a closed container or sealed plastic bag.

Spanish Crafts

Nacimiento

Materials

- Seven 2-inch clay flowerpots
- One 1 ½-inch clay flowerpot
- Seven 1 ½-inch wooden beads
- One ⅓-inch wooden bead
- Fabric scraps (felt, satin, cotton)
- Lace scraps (optional, for angel)
- Metallic wrapping paper (optional, for crowns)
- Fine-point felt-tip pens (for drawing faces)
- Low-temperature glue gun and glue sticks
- Excelsior (curled wood shavings) or other straw-like material for floor of stable

- Shoebox
- Pipe cleaners (gold, brown, white)
- Gift box, 2 inches x 3 inches
- Air-dry clay
- Light brown acrylic paint
- String, about 16 inches
- Four 1 ¾-inch Shaker pegs (or other small sticks for camel legs)
- Yellow/light brown yarn or embroidery thread
- Twig, about 6-inch (for Joseph's staff)—or may use brown pipe cleaner

Copy all patterns onto tracing paper. Cut them out along the solid black lines. (Be sure to stop where each line ends.)

D

Joseph, Mary, Three Wise Men, Washer Woman, Angel

To make bodies:

1. For each of the seven figures, trace pattern piece A onto fabric. Choose fabric appropriate for each character (white for angel, brown for Joseph, and so on). Cut out.

2. Stand flowerpot on its rim, so that the base of the flowerpot is now the top. Glue fabric around flowerpot, starting at base. (Overlap excess fabric at base, like petals of a flower.) Trim any excess fabric.

3. Trace pattern piece B onto fabric. (Make sure you use fabric that matches each figure.) Cut out. Glue onto base of flowerpot, which is now the top. Trim excess fabric.

4. Glue head (1 ½-inch wooden bead) to base.

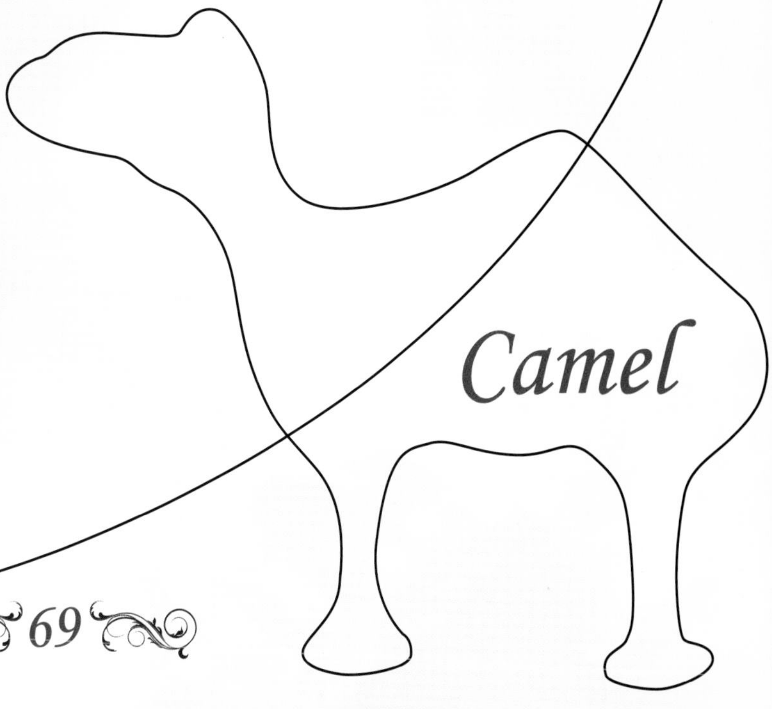

A

Camel

Finishing:

For Joseph, trace pattern piece C (headdress) onto fabric. Cut out. Glue to top of head, making sure to cover the hole in the bead. Glue twig to side of body (or cut piece of brown pipe cleaner into length of a long staff and glue to side of body).

For Mary, trace pattern piece D (veil) onto fabric. Cut out. Glue to top of head, covering the hole in the bead.

For Washer Woman, trace pattern piece E (head scarf) onto fabric. Cut out. Glue onto top of head, covering hole. Cut out pattern piece F (apron). Glue to front of body. Cut piece of string to fit and tie around waist.

For Wise Men, trace pattern piece G (crown) onto fabric or metallic wrapping paper. Cut out. Glue onto head. Decorate as desired.

For Angel, bend white pipe cleaners into wings. Glue to back of body. Glue yarn or embroidery thread to head to serve as hair. Bend a 5-inch section of gold pipe cleaner into a halo and glue into place on top of hair.

For all figures, use felt-tip pens to draw eyes and a mouth.

Baby Jesus

Draw a face on the ⅛-inch wooden bead. Glue the bead to the base of the 1 ½-inch flowerpot. Cut a 5-inch square piece of white or beige cloth and wrap the flowerpot so that only the head shows. Bend a piece of gold pipe cleaner about 3 inches long into a halo and glue onto head. Place small amount of excelsior (or other straw-like material) in gift box, and lay the Baby Jesus in the gift box.

Camel

Use air-dry clay to sculpt a camel. (You can use the shape provided as a guide.) Place four Shaker pegs into body as legs. Allow to dry completely, then paint light brown.

Star

Bend white pipe cleaner into shape of a star. If desired, trace fabric the size of the star, and glue onto star.

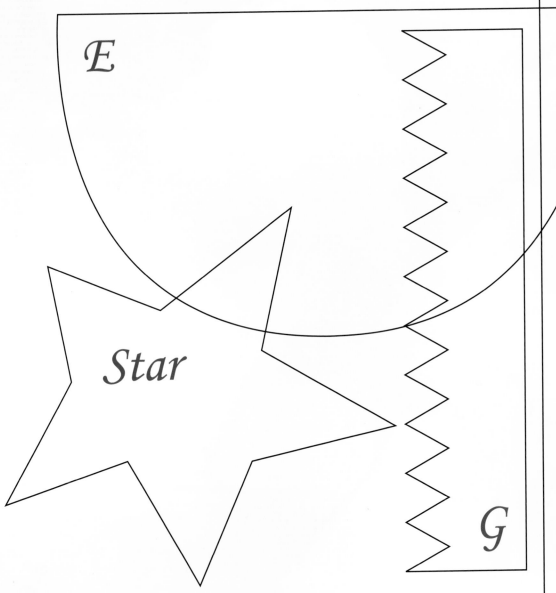

C

E

Star

G

Assembly

Lay shoebox on its side so that one long end forms the bottom of the stable and the other, the top. (You may want to use a colored felt-tip pen to draw "wooden planks" for the top of the stable or cover the stable with brown construction paper.) Spread excelsior (or other straw-like material) on floor of shoebox. Place Mary, Joseph, and the manger containing Baby Jesus in the stable. Stand angel atop stable. Glue star to one of the top/front corners of the stable. Arrange Wise Men, camel, and washerwoman nearby.

Guitar ornament

Materials

- Two small round buttons, each with four holes
- Two large round buttons with holes (one button should be slightly larger than the other)
- Two pipe cleaners
- Needle and bright-colored thread
- Scissors
- White glue
- Scrap of yarn or string

1. Lay out the pipe cleaners side by side and curl the ends, as shown, to form the top of the neck. Thread the needle with a length of thread about three times as long as a pipe cleaner. Knot one end of the thread. Put needle and thread aside for use in step 3.

2. Glue the small round button to the top of the neck, as shown. The large buttons form the guitar's body. Glue them in place as shown.

3. String your guitar with bright-colored thread before the glue dries on the buttons. With the guitar facing you, refer to the diagram below for the stringing sequence. Push the needle: from back to front in hole A; front to back in hole B; back to front in hole C; front to back in hole D. Secure with a knot at the back. Let the glue dry. Hang your guitar on the Christmas tree by means of a loop made of yarn or string.

1

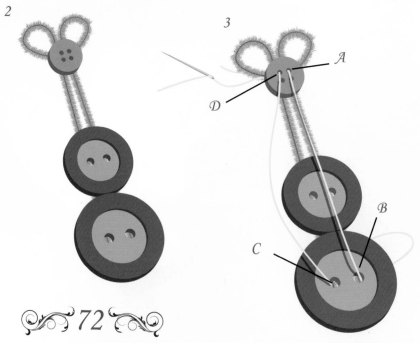

2

3

D

A

B

C

Zambomba ornament

The distinctive sound of a real *zambomba*—a type of drum—is made by moving the center stick up and down through the skin stretched over the top of the drum. Your toy *zambomba* will not make this sound. But the ornament will add an authentic Spanish touch to your Christmas tree.

Materials

- Paper or plastic drinking cup, preferably with lid
- Sheet of construction paper (if your cup has no lid)
- Scraps of Christmas wrapping paper
- Drinking straw
- Three pipe cleaners
- White glue
- Scissors
- Pencil
- Rubber band

1. If your cup has no lid, make one from construction paper. Place the top rim of the cup on a sheet of construction paper and trace around it. Then trace another circle around the first, adding a half-inch allowance all the way around. Cut out the larger circle. Clip the edges as shown and fold in toward the center.

2. Glue the lid in place. Fasten it with a rubber band until the glue is dry.

3. Cut a few strips of various wrapping papers. Make them long enough to encircle the cup and overlap at the edges. Smear a thin coat of glue on the sides of the cup and cover the cup with the colored paper. Extra glue may be needed for the overlapping edges. Let the glue dry.

4. Cut two strips of ringed paper long enough to overlap around the top of the cup. Curl the fringe with a pencil. Glue the fringed strips into place, and let the glue dry.

5. With sharpened pencil or scissors, punch three holes in the lid of your cup, as shown—one in the center, and a pair of holes about an inch apart near the edge. Cut a six-inch length of drinking straw. Place a drop of glue on the center hole of the lid. Insert the straw through the hole so that about four inches of straw stick out above the lid. Let the glue dry. As decoration, coil a pipe cleaner or two around the straw. Bend a pipe cleaner to form a loop for hanging the ornament. Put a drop of glue on each of the remaining holes in the lid. Push the ends of the pipe cleaner through the holes and let the glue dry.

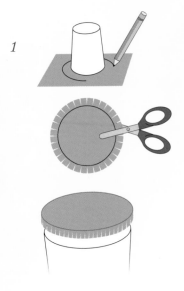

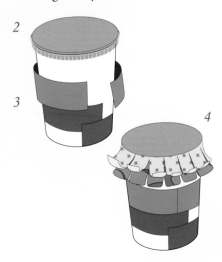

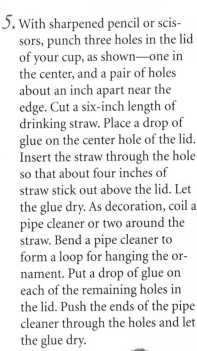

Spanish Melodies

En Belén Tocan a Fuego *(A Fire Is Started in Bethlehem)*

Andante

1. En Be - lén to - can a fue - go Del por - tal sa - len las lla - mas, Por - que
1. Here in Beth -le - hem this eve - ning, Springs a might-y Flame from Heav-en, Whom our

di - cen que ha — na - ci - do El Re - den - tor de las al - mas.
sin - ful - ness will be con - sum - ing, And through Whom we are for - giv-en

2. In a cold and humble stable,
   Blooms a spotless white Carnation,
   That becomes a lovely purple Lily,
   Sacrificed for our redemption.
   Refrain

3. Washing swaddling clothes for Jesus,
   Mary by a stream is singing.
   Birdlings chirp to her a joyful greeting,
   And the rippling brook is laughing.
   Refrain

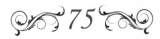

Fum, Fum, Fum (Foom, Foom, Foom)

Allegretto

1. ¡Vein - ti - cin - co de di - ciem - bre, Fum, fum, fum!
1. On De - cem - ber five and twen - ty, Foom, foom, foom!

¡Vein - ti - cin - co de di - ciem - bre, Fum, fum,
On De - cem - ber five and twen - ty, Foom, foom,

fum! Na - ci - do ha por nues - tro a - mor, El Ni - ño
foom! For the love of us is giv'n The ho - ly

Dios, el Ni - ño Dios; Hoy de la vir - gen Ma -
In - fant, Son of Heav'n, Of the Virg - in, Jo - seph's

ri - a En es - ta no - che tan fri - a, ¡Fum, fum, fum!
bride, To all the earth good will be - tid - ing, Foom, foom, foom!

2. Little birds from out the forest,
   Foom, foom, foom!
   Little birds from out the forest,
   Foom, foom, foom!
   All your fledglings leave behind,
   And seek the infant Savior kind,
   Come, and build a downy nest
   To warm the lovely Baby blessed,
   Foom, foom, foom!

3. Little stars up in the heavens,
   Foom, foom, foom!
   Little stars up in the heavens,
   Foom, foom, foom!
   If you see the Baby cry,
   O, do not answer with a sigh!
   Rather, lighten up the sky
   With Heav'n's beams of radiant brightness,
   Foom, foom, foom!

Campana Sobre Campo (Bells over Bethlehem)

Acknowledgments

Cover:

© Carlos Dominique, Alamy Images

2: © Rafa Rivas, AFP/Getty Images
6: © Dreamstime
8: © Jadwiga Lopez
9: © Marco Cristofori, Robert Harding World Imagery/Getty Images; © Jadwiga Lopez
10: © C. Zamora, Fotomax
11: © Maxine Hesse, Fotomax
12: © J. Buesa, Salmer Arte
13: © Ben Molyneux Spanish Collection/Alamy Images
14: © Maxine Hesse, Fotomax
15: AP Images
16: Salmer Arte
18: © Ana Abadia, age footstock
19: © Gastromedia/Alamy Images
20: © Jadwiga Lopez
21: © Maxine Hesse, Fotomax
22: AP Images
23: © Andrea Comas, Reuters/Landov
24: Salmer Arte
25: © Rafael Marchante, Reuters/Landov
26-27: © Jadwiga Lopez
28: © Maxine Hesse, Fotomax
29: © Jadwiga Lopez
30: Detail of *Saint Cecilia* by Michiel van Coxcie (1499-1592); Museo del Prado, Madrid, Spain (© Erich Lessing, Art Resource)
31: © Oso Media/Alamy Images
32: Hirmer Verlag
33: Sevilla Tourism Bureau
34: © Jadwiga Lopez
35: © Maxine Hesse, Fotomax
36: Detail of the *Nativity* (1597) oil on canvas by Federico Barocci; Museo del Prado, Madrid, Spain (© INTERFOTO/Alamy Images)
37: © C. Zamora, Fotomax
38: © Rafa Rivas, AFP/Getty Images
39: © Marmaduke St. John, Alamy Images
40-41: © Jadwiga Lopez
42: © Marco Cristofori, Robert Harding World Imagery/Getty Images
43: © Victor Fraile, Reuters/Landov
44-45: AP Images
47: © Felix Ordonez Ausin, Reuters/Landov
48: Detail of *The Adoration of the Magi* (14th century); Monasterio de Pedralbes, Barcelona, Spain (© Erich Lessing, Art Resource)
49: WORLD BOOK photo by Steve Hale
51: Salmer Arte
52-53: © Chen Haitong, Xinhua/Landov
54: © Felix Ordonez Ausin, Reuters/Landov
55: Spanish Tourist Office
56: © Bilderbox/age fotostock
57: Spanish Tourist Office
58: (top and middle) Museum of the Art of Catalonia, Barcelona; (bottom) Galdiano Museum, Madrid; (Giraudon)
60: *Adoration of the Shepherds* (1614) oil on canvas by El Greco; Museo del Prado, Madrid (Giraudon)
61: *Adoration of the Magi* (1619) oil on canvas by Diego Rodriguez Velázquez; Museo del Prado, Madrid, Spain (Giraudon)
62: © Travelshots/Alamy Images
64: © Cindy Miller Hopkins, Danita Delimont/Alamy Images
68-73: WORLD BOOK illustrations by Matt Carrington

Advent Calendar:

© Ricardo De Mattos, iStockphoto

Recipe Cards:

WORLD BOOK illustrations by Eileen Mueller Neill